Digitopia Blues

Digitopia Blues

Race, Technology, and the American Voice

JOHN SOBOL

NATIONAL LIBRARY OF CANADA CATALOGUING IN PUBLICATION DATA

Sobol, John, 1963–
Digitopia blues

Includes index.
ISBN 0-920159-89-3

1. African Americans—Music—History and criticism. 2. African Americans—Social conditions. 3. Popular music— United States—History and criticism. I. Title.
ML3479.S677 2002 780'.89'96073
C2002-910143-3

Cover and book design: Alan Brownoff
Printed and bound in Canada by Kromar Printing Ltd., Winnipeg, Manitoba.
Cover photograph of Billie Holiday © Bettman/CORBIS/MAGMA

The Banff Centre Press gratefully acknowledges the Canada Council for the Arts for its support of our publishing program.

The Banff Centre
for the Arts

BANFF CENTRE PRESS
Box 1020
Banff, AB Canada
T1L 1H5
www.banffcentre.ca/press

For Annie, Sophie, and Louis

Contents

ix *Acknowledgements*
xiii *Foreword*
xv *Prelude*

PART 1 Bluesology

3 CHAPTER 1
Chokamo

6 CHAPTER 2
Africa in America

14 CHAPTER 3
The Blues

17 CHAPTER 4
The River Widens

24 CHAPTER 5
From Bessie to Billie

32 CHAPTER 6
Lush Life

36 CHAPTER 7
Scat Singing

42 CHAPTER 8
Eddie Jefferson

45 CHAPTER 9
Slang and Jive

51 CHAPTER 10
A Love Supreme

55 CHAPTER 11
We Insist! Freedom Now Suite

PART 2 Printopolis

61 CHAPTER 12
The Forerunners of the New Bards

71 CHAPTER 13
Song of a Poet

73 CHAPTER 14
William Carlos Williams and the New World Idiom

80 CHAPTER 15
Beats and Riffs

84 CHAPTER 16
Rock 'n' Roll

91 CHAPTER 17
Word and Deed

102 CHAPTER 18
Black Poets on the Page

107 CHAPTER 19
Black Poets on the Stage

PART 3 Digitopia

117 CHAPTER 20
Hip Hop's Four Oral Elements

127 CHAPTER 21
Flippin' the Script

139 *Notes*
143 *Index*
153 *Permissions*

Acknowledgements

THIS BOOK HAS BEEN INFORMED by the wisdom and generosity of innumerable individuals. Family members, friends, and mentors have helped me throughout its composition, as have different artists and elders, many of whom I have never met. I feel blessed to have had access to so much strength and beauty.

I received unwavering support from my wife Annie Hillis, my parents Ken and Julie Sobol and my sisters Jane and Corry and their lovely families. My editor Kim Echlin offered many valuable insights and welcome encouragement. My copy editor Maureen Nicholson wielded her sharp blade judiciously and my publisher Lauri Seidlitz managed my meanderings and misgivings with admirable aplomb. Phil Spitzer and Don Stein were also instrumental in moving this book towards publication. To all of you I am very grateful.

I have been inspired and enlightened in exchanges with poets and musicians Paul Dutton, John Giorno, Cecil Taylor, Jayne Cortez, Jeannette Armstrong, Tim Lander, Jerome Rothenberg, Ivan Symonds, Mike Zwerin, Nick Ayoub, Danny Barker, Lillian Allen, Clifton Joseph, Bob Holman, bill bissett, Shirley Bear, Kate Hammett-Vaughn, Coat Cooke, Ron Samworth, Bobby Wiseman, Hugh Fraser, Guillermo Gómez-Peña, Fred Berry, Marshall Webb, Graham Kirkland, Tim Posgate, Tim Brady, George Lewis, Lisle Ellis, Michel Bruyere, Mike and

Kate Westbrook, Quincy Troupe, Barry Wallenstein, Sheila Jordan, Peter Valsamis, Joe Williams, Billy Eckstine, McCoy Tyner, M.Doughty, Jimmy Witherspoon, Professor Griff, Kalamu ya Salaam, Kathy Acker, René Lussier, Slim Gaillard, Steve Cannon, Tracie Morris, George Adams, Fortner Anderson, Robert Jodoin, Laszlo Gefin, Bob Mover and Andrew White, to name a few. We're lucky you are who you are (even you who are gone).

Many other gracious individuals have helped teach me my subject, including: Lewis Porter, Andrew Homzy, Sue Mingus, Patrick Darby, Roberto Sifuentes, Freddy Nyiti, Jane Jacobs, Irene Aebi, Montri Umavijani, David Findlay, Leo Feigin, Mike Donovan, Aaron Williamson, Werner Uelingher, Richard Armstrong, Sapphire, Daina Augaitis, and Carol Phillips.

Steve Lacy both encouraged and challenged me after reading this book when it was only three pages long. His respectful critique nourished me for a long time.

I owe a particular debt of gratitude to my two exceptionally talented poetic collaborators, Alex Ferguson and Kedrick James, with whom (as *AWOL Love Vibe*) I have been privileged to undertake outrageous adventures in improvised poetic orality.

I read many wonderful books during the course of my research. A handful of them transformed my vision of myself, my story, and my world. These include:

Walter J. Ong's definitive *Orality and Literacy*,
Julian Jayne's *The Origin of Consciousness in the Breakdown of the Bicameral Mind*,
Jerome Rothenberg's two-volume *Poems for the Millennium* and his earlier landmark anthology, *Technicians of the Sacred*,
Julio Finn's deep and defiant Hoodoo primer *The Bluesman*,
Bruce Chatwin's *The Songlines*,
Ben Sidran's prescient and under appreciated *Black Talk*,
Marshall McLuhan's *Gutenberg Galaxy*,
Alice Notley's tender and deep *Doctor Williams' Heiresses*,
Ishmael Reed's *Mumbo Jumbo*,
Brian Ward's *Just My Soul Responding: Rhythm and Blues, Black Consciousness and Race Relations*, and
Mezz Mezzrow's *Really the Blues.*

And I listened to a lot of music too. Music has been the anchor of my moral, cultural, and social life for many years. Listing all of the musicians who have blown my mind and elevated my spirit would take far too long, however. Instead I'd simply like to acknowledge my debt to them, and to express my gratitude.

I also explored several excellent repositories of artifacts and information during the course of my research: The Hogan Jazz Archive at Tulane University, Rutgers University's Institute of Jazz Studies, The Sound Archives of The British Library, The Library of Congress and The Duke Ellington Archive at The Smithsonian.

My ideas have been informed by the experiences and insights of all those whom I've mentioned, and by many others as well. The limitations of this book, however, are entirely my own. I wish to express my deepest gratitude for the respect and goodwill I have been shown, and for the opportunity to share this story that I have learned — and am still learning.

Foreword

THIS IS A STORY OF MYTHICAL VOICES, of abstract collective voices that exist in the realm of imagination — and yet speak and sing audibly in dialogue with events both great and small. It is also the story of real voices — my voice, your voice, our voices, their voices — voices that belong to real bodies and express real emotions and are the muscles of real souls. Here is a story of poetry that yearns for wholeness, for a unity of purpose and need that will unleash its transformative magic. And here too is the story of a poetry that is denied wholeness, that is stripped of unity, that adapts, and that refashions itself in music.

This book is about the search for the reconciliation of the body and the word in a literate world and the fate of poetry and people in the digital future. It is about technology. And about race. And about how the two are related. It is about how American musicians and poets have mapped that complex and violently contested matrix.

This is a vast story. Its scope extends far beyond the grasp of any one individual. Like traditional mythologies, it has innumerable access points and can be interpreted in many ways. My idiosyncratic take on this epic history is really a personal narrative. It is not comprehensive, not definitive, and emphatically not a reference book.

Why and how I arrived at my idiosyncratic conclusions — particularly with regard to race — will be important to some readers. And context is important to me, too. So let me briefly introduce myself.

Outside, my body says I'm white. My face, hair, and skin say I'm part Ashkenazi Jew, part Scot, part Irish, and maybe a bit French. And I suppose I'm those things inside, too. But I'm also a musician, and my music is mostly black. Inside, my heroes are black men and women like Rahsaan Roland Kirk and Dinah Washington. Like Al Green and Bob Marley. You should see my record collection. It's as black as I am white. So what exactly does that make me? A cultural appropriator? A wannabe? A bourgeois colonizer? A music lover? An explorer? An enthusiastic student? All of the above probably. And more.

Over the past twenty-five years of listening and playing, of working my way back through the history of black music, I've come to the conclusion that race is obviously crucial to the music (in the sense that black music was always made by and for black people), but there exists another dynamic that supersedes or at least parallels race, and that is *orality*. Many of the qualities that drew me to black music are characteristics of orality, of oral cultures. As such, those characteristics are shared to varying degrees by other oral cultures around the world. Collectively, Africans and their diasporic descendants possess an idiomatic musical vocabulary that is remarkable for its breadth, subtlety, and passion. They share this vocabulary, however, not simply because of their black skin, but largely because of their powerful adherence to a vital oral mindset.

Thus, in passing through the kalaidoscopic tunnel of black communication, I was invited to resurrect my own latent orality — to discover my own experience, my own expression, and my own poetry. That knowledge has opened up inspiring new worlds and engendered deep relationships. And for me it all began with music, with black music, as it did for all of us long ago, intertwined like goat fibre wound round the world-body of a beating drum.

Prelude

Notes for a Mythology of the Voice

Ohhh, unnhhhh, oooohhh, unnnhhh, ohhh, ahh, ahhh, ahhhh,
ahhhhhhhhhhhh...

He shivered when she made that sound
His blood rushed when she warbled like that
He tried blindly to answer
The moon at night came to life in her
This was in a cave in a desert on a plain, a long, long time ago

She walked and she walked and she walked
As she walked she sang to her unborn child
She sang of walking and of bearing a child
She sang that the child should hear her and be comforted
And she walked slowly, the weight of her belly drawing her from
side to side with each small step
Her breath came shorter as she sang

And she heard the echo of her song deep inside herself, in her bones,
in her belly, in the movement of her listening twin
She sang to herself and for herself in her own voice
And she listened

in love

He was four when he first saw his uncle stumble drunkenly across the room, babbling incoherently. Once he tugged his mother's hand and asked, "Mama, where do our voices come from?"

Now he is seven, and he watches proudly as his father cleans his gun: "Papa, when you shoot someone, I'm gonna write a song about it."

And in his dreams he hears voices. Sometimes they sing. Sometimes they cry. Sometimes they call to him in a language he does not understand

Sometimes he walks to the river and listens to its sounds and sucks his tongue around in his mouth full of spit to speak with the rushing river

Sometimes he walks in the snow and listens to its crunching beneath his boots, and he grinds his hard, white teeth together in time with the crunch crunch

Later, when he is old enough to hunt alone, and he has learned all the songs of his family, and all the songs of the river and of the snow, he leaves to learn more songs.
He walks. As he walks he sings, and as he walks he sings of all that he sees. All that is new. His footsteps echo with the songs of his passing, and the land rejoices in his singing. His hair is long and

matted. He sings to strangers, but they shun his depths. He invents songs for each of them; the swift and the slow alike, the eager and the unglued.

He walks on.

He walked until he came to the edge of the world, and from beyond the edge of the world came a song. He sat and listened to the song. He listened for seven days and nights. It was an old song. One of the oldest. On the seventh night, he remembered the song. He had heard it as a child, in his dreams. As he listened, the moon and the traffic slipped away until he was alone, utterly alone with the song. Until he was the singer. This is what he sang:

> Water went they say. Land was not they say. Stones were not when water went they say. Cars were not they say. Drugs were not they say. Guns were not they say. America was not they say. Needles were not they say. People were washed away they say. Skyscrapers were washed away they say. Subways were washed away they say. Trees were washed away they say. Pigeons were not then they say. Muggers were not they say. Stretch limos were not they say. Money was not they say. Cops were not they say. Then telephones were not they say. Then newspapers were not they say. Then the Manhattan, the Brooklyn Bridges were not they say. The past was not they say. The wind was not they say. Then snow was not they say. Then rain was not they say. Then it didn't thunder they say. The trees were not when it didn't thunder they say. It didn't lighten they say. The clouds were not they say. Smog was not they say. It didn't appear they say. Words were not they say. It was very dark.

When the song was over, he sat for seven more days and nights. He was listening to the echo of the song, and he saw how all of his songs were echoes of this first song. He heard the echo of the river in the echo of this dream song. He heard the echo of his uncle's terrible cries. He heard the echo of his mother's lullabies. And he followed the sound of the echo beyond himself, beyond time, beyond the sea. He sailed out past the edge of the world and swam in the sound that played with death like a feather. The song was alive with fire, and the fire sounded all about him and he laughed as he inhaled the singing flame. And again he slept in the womb of song. And the whispering ghosts of singers past and future watched over him as he slept, alone, beneath the big-city bridge, in the flimsy, corrugated night.

PART 1

Bluesology

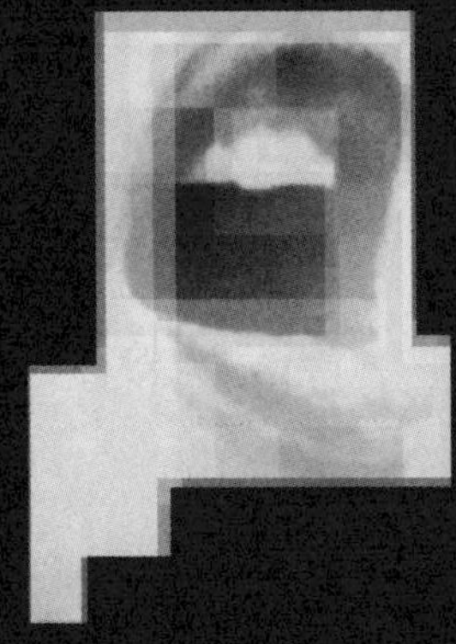

1

Chokamo

In the spring of 1989, I travelled to New Orleans for the first time. Within minutes of my arrival in the French Quarter, I'd been fleeced by a couple of fast-talking cons. Within an hour, I'd heard the world's sweetest alto saxophone sound, flung like honey from a lonely-eyed vestibule. I found myself awash in music, lost amid a tangled swamp of leathery voices, enthralled by half-forgotten stories and still-vital wisdom sunk in the Mississippi mud like a fat-bellied crocodile. And one sweaty afternoon, I found myself at the home of banjo player Danny Barker, one of the grand old men of New Orleans.

Danny Barker had played with the likes of Louis Armstrong and Cab Calloway as a young man, and Dr. John and Wynton Marsalis as an old man. He was born in 1909 into New Orleans's famed Barbarin family, which had birthed dozens of the century's greatest jazz musicians. He was married to blues diva Blue Lou Barker, whose singing I knew from an old LP called *Women of the Blues — The 1930s.* As I sat in Danny Barker's cozy bungalow drinking lemonade made by Blue Lou, and listened to the banjo-playing man hitch up his belt and spin his weary tales in a slow southern drawl, I knew I'd come to the right place. I heard the music talking. I was all ears.

That same year, The Belle Stars, a flash-in-the-pan British girl-group, hit the charts with their cover version of a wickedly catchy song called

"Iko Iko," featured on the soundtrack of the movie *Rain Man*. Two years earlier, a different version of "Iko Iko" sung by The Dixie Cups was featured on the soundtrack of another popular film, *The Big Easy*. For a while in the late 80s, the tune was on everyone's lips. Its curious call-and-response refrain goes:

> Talking 'bout
> hey now, *hey now*
> hey now, *hey now*
> Iko-iko-anday
> Jacomo fino ananay
> Jacomo fina nay

When The Dixie Cups recorded "Iko Iko" in 1965, the song hit No. 15 on the R & B charts. And yet the girl group had never planned to record "Iko Iko" at all. As Dixie Cup Barbara Hawkins remembers: "We were just clowning around with it during a session using drumsticks on ashtrays. We didn't realize that Jerry [Leiber] and Mike [Stoller] had the tapes running." "Iko Iko" was a song the girls had known as kids growing up in New Orleans. Barbara remembers learning it from her mother, who probably learned it from "Jockamo" James Crawford, who recorded it in 1950. Even his wasn't the first recorded version. Danny Barker had recorded the song with Blue Lou way back in 1933, but as Barker explained to me that lazy afternoon, the song's origins were far older still:

> I did four sides, two records. "Chocko Ma Fendo Hey," "My Indian Red," "Tutuma Is a Big Fine Thing," and "Coreen Died on a Battlefield." Those were Indian songs I knew when I was a kid. Nowadays, they done changed it around. And they don't say Chocko-mo, they say Yacomo. And I get very annoyed with it, because they don't study it ... Chockomo was an Indian song. Indians was masking. See Indians been masking for years. See at blacks' carnivals, blacks put [on] masks, they burlesque themselves. Anything funny ... some of 'em would mask in skeletons. You see 'em coming down the street. Fifteen or twenty skeletons. Tall guys, black suits, white paint, you know. And they'd make their own skulls out of papier mâché. And you see that, man, it scare the shit out of some people. And the blacks masked as

Indians, because they were proud of the Indians. In this country, the both of them were kicked around. One was kicked around like a football, an' the other was a punching bag. You know what they did to the Indians, shit. So they was both of them in the same boat...

Well, the blacks are masking as Indians. And a lot of Indians masqueraded as blacks. They come over [to] the blacks. They don't want to go on the reservation, so they change their name. He cuts his hair, he wore the clothes of the blacks. And took off that leather they used to use, fine leather, soft shammy-like. And he got rid of his mannerisms and got him a black woman, and he cool. Or an Indian woman got her a black man. And the census, the marshal, comes to check out how many Indians in the neighbourhood. They come around and say, "Any Indians living around here? See any Indians living around here?" Say, nope. Man'd be talking to an Indian, but the Indian done changed his makeup altogether. "No, I don't know. I ain't got time. I'm busy man."

So they had to make songs (the blacks masquerading as Indians) that them Indians sang. And the words the Indians used. Chockoma means to eat or drink. The Indians got a drink called Chock. Findo means, when you have a bowel movement. Findo. Jacomo. Eat my shit. That's what that means. Yeah, Chockamo findo hey! [sings] Chockamo findo hey, you son of a bitch, you. That's what you tell all the other Indians, y'understand. When they meet, one gang meet another gang, so they be singing them suggestive nasty songs. [sings] Chockamo findo hey, we gonna set on 'em, fuck 'em all up on Mardi Gras day. Like the one gang to another. But the average person don't know that. So that's a Mardi Gras song. Indian songs. In the public domain. Ain't nobody knows who wrote 'em. Neville Brothers and others around here they take 'em and add some other words to them and put their names on as writers. But they don't belong to no one.[1]

There's always more to black American music than meets the eye or the ear. There's always history, stretching back four hundred years, stretching like a dust-caked cry from the new world to the old.

2 Africa in America

AFRICA WAS, IS, AND ALWAYS WILL BE AN ORAL WORLD. West Africa, in particular, has been shaped by the imperatives of the living voice and not — as was the case with the colonial cultures that mutilated countries and voice in the seventeenth, eighteenth and nineteenth centuries — by the imperatives of the infallible, inanimate text.

Orality is functional. Art for art's sake makes no sense in Africa. Self-expression is not an end in itself but is always a form of communication.

Orality is public. Windows and doors are open. Sound travels. There are always ears. The more listeners the better. Each blade of grass whispers to the other.

Orality is communal. Creativity + Community = Communion. We are here, we are *hear*, we are. We share. Identity. Land. Language. Values. Needs. We reaffirm — we *re-create* — our community in sound, in song.

Orality is participatory. We dance. We shout out. We call, and the leader responds. We let you know what we think of your song. We add our own verses. We sing along. We dance. We drum. We dance.

Orality is interdisciplinary. What is music? There is only our joy, our worship, our pain, in body, in sound, in paint, clay, or bone. You do not dance without music. You cannot have music without dance. See the way I shift my hip in time as Fela chimes from my transistor radio? Do you see how the spirit moves me? Let me tell you a story. Let me sing you a song.

Orality is experiential. Sound dies as it is born on our lips. The experience — the creative moment — is what matters. The product is the process. Don't look for me in a museum. If I am in a museum, I am dead. I am a continuum. I am to be continued. I *am* not, I *become.*

Orality is vocal. I am the drum. I am a talking drum. My voice is your voice. My language is your language. Let us converse. I am the drummer's song, the fiddler's song, the xylophone's song. I am a song sung in the voice of my friend, the earth-fashioned instrument. I am a song.

This is how Cameroonian Francis Bebey describes the relationship of the human voice and the musical instrument:

> Vocal music is truly the essence of African musical art. This fact in no way diminishes the interest of musical instruments; on the contrary, since the prime motive of the instruments is to reconstitute spoken or sung language, they have a significance which is unparalleled in the music of other continents.[2]

The bel canto voice, according to the *Everyman Dictionary of Music,* sings in the "traditional Italian manner, with beautiful tone, perfect phrasing, clean articulation." In other words, the bel canto voice — the European classical musical voice — is defined in absolutes. *There is a right way and a wrong way to sing.* African vocal techniques bear no resemblance to bel canto and as a result were long perceived to be primitive by westerners who came in contact with them. Now that Eurocentric cultural imperialism has begun to break up (not least because the appropriation and exploitation of African-American singing styles has made many a fortune for white rock stars and thereby "legitimized" those styles), the techniques of African singing are beginning to be appreciated by non-Africans for what they are: an entirely different singing aesthetic. Here's Francis Bebey again, on the gulf between western and African sensibilities:

> The objective of African music is not necessarily to produce sounds agreeable to the ear, but to translate everyday experiences into living sound. In a musical environment whose constant purpose

> is to depict life, nature or the supernatural, the musician wisely avoids using beauty as his criterion because no criterion could be more arbitrary.[3]

Orality is playful. Words open like windows, doors, winds, inviting, questioning, challenging, riddling, teasing, prodding, deflecting. Orality avoids fixed data in favour of a momentary recreation of reality, a redefinition of one self in dialogue with another self.

Years ago, my friend Joe Delaney, a Canadian of Irish descent, went to visit his relatives in Northern Ireland for the first time. Arriving alone from the airport in a cab, he was distressed to find nobody home. The street was deserted. He was a stranger, and his backpack made him feel self-conscious. The barbed wire and paramilitary murals sparked his morbid imagination. A car occupied by a few young men drove slowly past him on the narrow street. Then it drove slowly past him going the other way. Joe was genuinely scared. The car stopped and a young, tough-looking Irishman peered at him. Joe braced for flight. Then a voice rang out: "Do they call you Joe?" It was his cousin, Paddy, and Joe sighed with profound relief.

The point is that the oralist — Irish or Bantu — isn't interested in fixed facts. The question wasn't "Are you Joe?" Instead, it was an open-ended question, one that offered a variety of interpretations. Who are *they*? Who is Joe? Who's asking? *Why* do they call you Joe?

African orality constantly makes use of this circumlocutory approach, which has been called *indirection*. The power of the indirect statement lies in forcing the listener to do his or her own work, to actively make the connections between tangentially connected images or ideas. And it works, because the collision of ideas in one's own brain will always be more stimulating, and therefore more accessible, than information that requires little inner assembly. As Ben Sidran says in his book *Black Talk*, " The direct statement is considered crude and unimaginative; the veiling of all contents in ever-changing paraphrase is … the criterion of intelligence."[4]

Malcolm X would have agreed: "I am not a Politician, nor the son of a Politician, I am not a Republican, nor a Democrat, nor an American."[5] What is Malcolm X implying? What *is* he then? He is the descendant of Africans in America, and he is in the process of *becoming*. His ancestors were slaves, and their ancestors were Africans. His lineage is inescapably oral.

The gulf between oral and literate values cannot be overestimated. Literate value arises when knowledge is abstracted from context and embedded in literate artifacts. Literate economies, for example, are based on the manipulation of impersonal products whereas oral economies are based on the maintenance of relationships. Gift-giving is a prime example of a relationship-based economic tool used widely in oral societies around the world. In a society ruled by literate tools, however, in which possession of a legal deed is an absolute assertion of ownership and status, the need to maintain healthy relationships with one's neighbours in order to ensure one's place within a community is eliminated. Gift-giving is thus economically irrelevant in a literate society.

On almost every level, oral values stand in opposition to literate values. Orality favours process over product, event over artifact, subjectivity over objectivity, practice over theory, intuition over analysis, the collective over the individual, spoken over written words, social function over personal expression, improvisation over reproduction.

These opposing value systems have battled it out in countless cultures, economies, and psyches over the past five hundred years, and to a lesser extent in the two millennia before Gutenberg's invention of movable type. The battle has often been bloody. Literacy always conquers. Orality is always conquered *because literacy is more efficient, and evolution rewards efficiency.* But orality is never eradicated. The human psyche does not easily abandon the tools with which it has shaped itself over countless millennia. Members of cultures that haven't fully internalized literate values continue to think and act differently than predominantly literate peoples.

What happened to the African oral identity in America? What happened to the words, the languages, the songs of Africans sold into slavery in the New World — to the voices that sang of a familiar community life, history, and land — when they were shipped to a brutal new world and stripped of their ancient referents? A folk song recorded in 1967 by Jamaican rocksteady stars The Melodians, and featured on the movie soundtrack for *The Harder They Come*, offers one answer, couched in Old Testament metaphor:

By the rivers of Babylon
where we sat down
and there we wept
when we remembered Zion.
For the wicked
carried us away
Captivity required from us a song
How can we sing King Alfa's song
in a strange land?[6]

The African voice in America was distorted and disguised. It was physically restricted by the prohibition of African languages, formally abused by the eradication of traditional subject matter, and spiritually assailed by the suppression of African religious activities among slaves. The power of the word was a constant threat to slave owners. Allow slaves to talk, and they might plot. Allow them to sing in Dogon or Yoruban, and they might begin to hope. Allow them to invoke their gods, and all hell might break loose. For generations of slaves, America meant more than physical slavery. Slavery eliminated the coherence of African community life. It made the songs that maintained that coherence irrelevant. Denied their languages, slaves were denied a past. Denied literate education, they were denied a future. And yet there was always — at least — the present, in which the word, in whatever fluid form it could afford to take, offered comfort and communion. For although slaves were forced to abandon their traditional songs, their oral orientation toward the world could not be so easily dismissed. Slaves could not be stopped from singing.

Work songs reverberated wherever and whenever slaves worked. Often a leader was chosen to set the pace in song as a team of men or women hoed rows, broke rocks, hammered ties, threshed corn, picked cotton, loaded bales, sawed wood, felled trees, washed linen, drove mules, or hauled water, all the while chiming in on cue, keeping time, sharing the weight, making isolated exertion into an expressive dialogue, a communal moment, one part of a greater, better whole.

Field hollers rang across fields as men and women working alone let out a personal cry, a unique wail that was theirs alone, a long and deep exhalation of identity in sound, distinct from all others, a solitary affirmation of self, honed and shaped through the years, echoing among the rocks and brambles like a wandering ghost. That cry asserted faith in the moment, releasing tension, giving a soul strength to carry on.

Spirituals resounded in churchly choirs as ever-greater numbers of slaves (and eventually ex-slaves) adopted the forms of Christian worship, raising the roof in collective song, refashioning psalms and hymns, embracing metaphor with a conviction born of necessity, adapting the oppressor's language to their own needs, dreaming of salvation, imbuing white religion with the African spirit.

The black preacher, "the man of words," used both verbal and body language to inspire and enthuse his flock. He called on more than God's name, actively invoking God's presence at the urging of his congregation, which was physically and spiritually possessed by the divine spirit. This Christian shaman was almost purely African. For just as the collective experience is of paramount importance in African creative expression, so in African religious expression is the act of participatory communal worship the essence of the spiritual event. At the turn of the twentieth century, W.E.B. Du Bois argued that nineteenth-century black Americans never really assimilated the Christianity of their white oppressors. He believed that despite the popularity of Christianity among slaves and their descendants, black Americans remained alienated and excluded from the religion that claimed to offer salvation and guidance to the weak and innocent but in reality condoned the barbarous institution that had kept them enchained. According to Du Bois, Christianity was embraced by an ever-increasing percentage of the black population in America during the nineteenth century, predominantly as an arena in which to express, explore, and celebrate the full emotional and creative spectrum denied to its marginalized adherents in everyday life. Though the typical nineteenth-century black Christian service was clearly essentially African, with its improvised antiphony, its propulsive music, its guttural cries and wails, its speaking in tongues, its trances, its public ecstasies, Africa was never acknowledged by congregants as a source of its spiritual power. Rather, it was the Christian trinity — the Father, the Son and the Holy Ghost — to whom the spiritual power of the African-American religious service was attributed.

In contrast to black America's socially acceptable Christian worship, hoodoo songs were prayers to West African deities, to the spirits of the *loas* and *orishas*, to Ogun, Shango, Legba, and many more. Hoodoo emerged in the southern U.S. during slavery as a sibling of Cuban

Santeria, West Indian obeah, Haitian voudoun, and Brazilian *Candomblé*, all localized, hybrid versions of ancient West African religions. In the U.S., as elsewhere in the New World, hoodoo was taboo, and its songs were profoundly subversive. They were thrilling, whispered in the fugitive silence of the deep bush, in the darkness of the secret stump, in the shadow of the mossy bayous. These invocative songs delivered fear and faith; the possibility of resistance; the importance of not becoming one of *them* and reasserted trampled identities; values and beliefs reinforced by the conjuring root doctor with his talismans and charms, his *mojos* and *wangas*, and his deep herb lore.

As one former slave recalled in an account quoted by Julio Finn in his book *The Bluesman*, "Religious services among slaves were strictly forbidden. But the slaves would steal away into the woods at night and hold services. They would form a circle on their knees around the speaker who would also be on his knees. He would bend forward and speak over or into a vessel of water to drown out the sound. If anyone became animated or cried out, the others would quickly stop the noise by placing their hands over the offender's mouth."[7]

This image — of the slave determined to celebrate his or her faith, yet physically silenced and worshipping secretly in desperate fear — perfectly represents the oppression of African orality and identity, whose essence — unrestricted public affirmation of community life in word and song — had been outlawed. Thus both hoodoo and black Christianity were shaped by denial and subterfuge. Hoodoo celebrated its African spiritual heritage but was forced to scrape out a shadowy, underground existence. Christianity operated in the light of day, yet the soulful source of its transformative power remained hidden. In each case, the magical power of the invocative voice was essential yet restricted. Both hoodoo and Christianity offered spiritual inspiration, but neither could rejoin the severed halves of the African psyche.

Such was the essential spiritual dilemma of the African in America: one could have a voice without the true word, or truthful words without a voice.

This book is about black America's collective quest to overcome that dilemma, to redeem its oral heritage; a quest that led through the blues, scat singing, jive talk, and R & B; through bebop, free jazz, gospel, and hip hop; through the voices of generations of oralists negotiating the contested territory of language in a hostile, literate world.

It is also the story of how and why American poets who were not black were drawn to black music, and what they learned from it as they moved ever closer to liberating themselves from the confines of the book. But this is not only the story of the past, of the racialized clash between oralists and literates in the twentieth century. It is also about the present and the future. It is the story of how oralists and literates are both being transformed into digitalists, and about the implications of that transformation on the struggle for economic equality being waged by marginalized communities in North America and around the world.

3 The Blues

> The road less travelled is the blues. Walk it to the ends of the earth. Stopping to make conversation or love in a small cabin. Singing to new ears every day. Always the same old tunes with a new verse or two thrown in. The blues for a good meal. An old guitar and songs about the meanest mistreater of them all, sister fate.

WHEN A COMMUNITY IS FUNCTIONING PROPERLY, it teaches its members, or rather they teach each other, to value themselves and their relationships with each other, with their history, with their world. They show their affection without irony, apology, or embarrassment. Their songs are of an *unyielding* love. In America, the slave's need to express her love of life and community in song remained powerful. But the love itself was gashed. The American slave couldn't feel the love that binds a fully enfranchised member to a just community. The African in her couldn't sing those songs of celebration and achievement, of history and ancestry, of courtship and marriage that were her heritage. In the middle of such a song, the bride and groom might be sold off to different plantations, or worse. *Le droit du seigneur* and the lynching tree would make any wedding party uneasy.

The will to love was still present in America's slaves, as it must be in any people determined to survive oppression. And the need to express love in song also remained present. But during slavery — and afterward — the traditional affirmative subjects were prohibited or irrelevant. So the subjects became negative, and the songs became songs of pain and hurting. The singers sang of the grief their community was subject to, omitting nothing, least of all their own misery. The sorrow that overtook Robert Johnson when he sang "Hellhound on My Trail" is naked, unhidden. But so too is his determination not to succumb to its pain. The song is an expression of love, of a love for himself and his world that cannot be trammelled by offence. It is the combination of unyielding love with unbearable pain that spurs the blues voice to such heart-rending emotion. The blues singer's voice — ferociously intense, extracting the most visceral truths from the debris of existence, threatening to explode each syllable with an incalculable attention to detail, rising, falling, trembling, reaching, spinning — life's song sung with the purest conviction. Unyielding love and unbearable pain.

The blues are a human voice. Not a fancied-up voice, not a trained voice, but an everyday voice heightened with just enough music to bring potent lyrics fully to life. Blues singers' singing voices are extremely close to their speaking voices, and the result is a powerful immediacy. Blues lyrics are relentlessly poetic and fully meet Ezra Pound's excellent definition of great literature: *language charged with meaning to the utmost possible degree.* The art of the blues lyricist is to create a set of images that are given meaning by the listener with an adventurous leap of the imagination. That connective act is both exciting and engaging, creating a poetic capacity in even the least "artistic" listener. Ultimately, the blues are a temporary emotional zone where passion and compassion commingle freely, bonding a community in sensual harmony.

Novelist Ralph Ellison was an enthusiastic witness to and chronicler of the transformative power of the blues. He grew up in the magical and magnetic musical outpost of Kansas City in the 20s and 30s. As a young man, he was friendly with the likes of Lester Young, Ben Webster, and Count Basie. Ellison's pals played with Bennie Moten's territory band, the Blue Devil Orchestra, before striking out on their own, and he regularly attended their dances. In the voice of the Blue Devils' legendary blues shouter, Jimmy Rushing — a.k.a. Mr. 5 x 5 — Ellison heard the vitality of black America expressed in song. Ellison also heard more clearly than many the echo of African community:

> Heard thus ... it was easy to imagine the voice as setting the pattern to which the instruments of the Blue Devil Orchestra and all the random sounds of night arose, affirming as it were, some ideal native to the time and land ... It was when Jimmy's voice began to soar with the spirit of the blues that the dancers — and the musicians — achieved that communion which was the true meaning of the public jazz dance.[8]

4 The River Widens

THE BLUES GAVE BIRTH TO JAZZ — as did ragtime, creole New Orleans, Congo Square dances, jug bands, tubas, trumpets and brass bands, clave rhythms, Storyville whorehouses, Buddy Bolden, Jelly Roll Morton, indian drums, and the bodies and dreams of innumerable Americans swaying to blue sound. To this day, you can have blues without jazz, but you can't have jazz without the blues.

The history of jazz is also profoundly intertwined with the history of recording technology. We have a record of jazz. We have jazz records. And so despite its essential evanescence, jazz has been lifted out of time, fixed, replicated, and fetishized, which is not necessarily a bad thing. Recording technology has given us a unique opportunity to assess the entire history of the music as it was played, as it is still played today, every time we put on a CD featuring Sidney Bechet or Ben Webster or Sun Ra. We can look back and say that jazz took a big step in 1919 when a bunch of white kids were hired to make the first jazz recording as the Original Dixieland Jazz Band. And here in 1923, when Bessie Smith first recorded "Downhearted Blues." And in 1925, when Louis Armstrong recorded with his Hot Sevens and Hot Fives. It's all here. The life of a music. On the shelf. Let us reap the benefit. Let us take advantage of this tool, not to catalogue and footnote, but to understand what the music is — and has always been — about.

One ear
Two ears
One hears
Two hear
She hears
We hear
They hear
Two ears
From here
To ear
And ear
To there
Two ears
To hear
Where here
And there
Will be
What key
From C to C
And then
What beat
When two
Ears meet
Two drummer's
Feet
One ear
Two ears
Whose 88 gears
Are black
And blue
And milk-white too
Though black
And white
Can both
Be blue
In jazz
No one
Is true

But blue
One blue
Two blues
This tune
Is dues
To the
All blues muse
Whose ears
Are smears
And eyes
Are tears
And face
Is the fear
Of losing
Her ears
And the joy
Of having
Them here
She hears
We hear
One ear
Two ears

Jazz as Sound

> When I know a man's sound, well, to me, that's him, that's the man. That's the way I look at it. Labels I don't bother with.
>
> —JOHN COLTRANE

Nothing in jazz is as important as an individual musician's sound. Nothing so readily identifies a jazz musician as the sound produced from his or her instrument. Classical musicians use the word *timbre*, but *sound* means so much more than that in the jazz lexicon. A jazz musician's sound is a personal icon, a carefully honed and sculpted voice through which he or she speaks. The spectrum of sounds produced by a thousand classical trumpeters in concert is likely to be narrower than that produced by any two jazz trumpeters.

The jazz musician's sound transcends every other aspect of jazz. It is the medium of the musician's imminent communication. Even jazz rhythm — called *swing* — which is generally believed to originate in the passage of a series of notes over a series of beats, is derived first and foremost from the attack with which each note is delivered. And that attack depends entirely upon the musician's timbral conception, or sound. In jazz — as in African music — rhythm follows sound; it follows the voice.

When a young musician begins to play jazz (or so it was before the growth of harmony-centred academic jazz programs), he or she begins searching for an identity in sound. If that sound is to be successful in representing the musician's individuality, then it must be as unique as he or she is. (Legendary altoist Maceo Parker, whose sweet honk is as identifiable as the Eiffel Tower, learned to play his saxophone one note at a time. Literally. "I practised one note over and over until it sounded like I wanted it to, then I'd move on to the next one," he once explained to me.) A jazz musician's sound is an inner voice sucked from a secret soul and spit out into the world.

But a jazz sound does not — cannot — exist in isolation. It comes to life only when its owner is present and has something to say. A jazz sound is always brimming with meaning, with function, with purpose. It is responsive to its context, adapting itself to the needs of the moment. It is constantly created and recreated in the image of its owner, whose skilled handling is based on a sophisticated understanding of an idiom whose expressive ideals remain rooted in such African oral principles as indirection. Instead of hitting a note straight on, jazz musicians will often slide up to a note, or growl it, or slur, bite, crack, ghost, or even omit it. The jazz vocabulary includes all these techniques and many more. They are all ways of charging a personal sound with meaning. They are the musical equivalent of what Wittgenstein called *significant tone*, and what Ben Sidran called *intonation contouring*. The point of these terms is that the meaning of a statement is not exclusively, or even primarily, its logical or harmonic content. In jazz, meaning is above all conveyed by tone.

Jazz as Conversation

The first principle of jazz is: mean what you say. You cannot lie to the music. It won't let you. It is possible to play insincere music, but when it's insincere, it's not jazz. It's something else, because the insecurities that cause insincerity are themselves purged by playing jazz. If you're angry, caught in a tight spot, you messed up and you know it and you're looking for a way out, you can go to the music and make your peace with it. But don't lie. Only by telling the truth can you be saved.

Very little attention has been paid to the crucial fact that the origin of the call-and-response technique lies in conversation. *Jazz consists of a series of interwoven conversations.* Recognizing this fact implies an even more significant revelation: jazz is based on oral forms. Jazz is oral poetry, not just metaphorically speaking, but idiomatically, structurally, and functionally. This conclusion runs counter to the prevailing notion that the key formal characteristics of jazz are derived from European influences.

African antiphony — call and response — promotes popular participation in the creative process, regulates the relevance of the leader's contribution, and provides an experiential model of social integration. Familiarity with the call-and-response technique was one of two key elements that allowed early jazz musicians to master collective improvisation. The other was the polyrhythmic legacy of African music, which is itself an extension of antiphony.

Jazz is full of legendary conversations, including the classic dialogues between Bessie Smith and Louis Armstrong, Lester Young and Billie Holiday, Dizzy Gillespie and Roy Eldridge, Gerry Mulligan and Chet Baker, Miles Davis and Gil Evans, Bill Evans and Scott LaFaro, Julius Hemphill and Oliver Lake. But these conversations are only a few among innumerable such expressive exchanges. Every jazz drummer worth his or her salt offers a running commentary on the proceedings in which they play a central part, articulating instant percussive responses to the conversational gambits of bandmates. Even big bands engage in moderated conversations, in which entire sections conduct extended dialogues. Duke Ellington was a master at devising cozy settings in which his band members could converse. And how his men could talk! Tricky Sam Nanton, Lawrence "Butter" Brown, Cootie Williams, Roy Nance, Johnny Hodges, Ben Webster, Sonny Greer, Sam Woodyard. Duke's men were masters of the plunger, the glissando, the undertone, the growl. They possessed a vast collective vocabulary of expressive oralisms, which provided them with a descriptive language of tremendous potency. And they used it to talk.

In the late 50s and 60s, the music of jazz innovators like Cecil Taylor and Ornette Coleman was characterized by simultaneous improvised overlapping conversations. This development, vilified by white cultural arbiters — and many established black jazzmen — as charlatanism, as pathological, was clearly different — and threatening. *Free jazz*, as the form came to be known, was called into being at a time in American history when black voices had begun shouting loudly for attention. But Ornette wasn't simply imitating or reflecting what was happening around him as the civil rights movement gained steam. Ornette's music *was itself* the embodiment and expression of the conflicted social dynamics working themselves out on jazz musicians and their communities.

The conversational mode in jazz has sometimes been elevated to such a sophisticated degree that it recreates the linguistically comprehensible conversations of African instrumentalists. Brian Priestly quotes Charles Mingus explaining that Mingus and Eric Dolphy "used to really talk and say words with our instruments ...We had different 'conversations,' we'd discuss our fear, our life, our views of God, which is still our main subject today."[9] I'd like to relate an anecdote told to me by a friend who frequently heard Mingus and Dolphy play in New York clubs. He was at a table with the two musicians as they carried on a conversation between sets. When the musicians went back to play, they remarked that they'd continue their conversation on stage. Mingus and Dolphy then played a set featuring extensive interaction between the bassist and reed man. When the set ended, my friend asked Mingus how the conversation had ended. Mingus told him. My friend then asked Dolphy, in another part of the room, the same question. To his astonishment, he received an almost identical reply.

Skeptics will have their explanations. But remember the talking drum. Mingus and Dolphy shared an African way of knowing.

Jazz as Story

Jazz is made up of more than conversations. Jazz is also a compendium of stories. Every instrumental solo — at least every successful one — is a narrative tale with a beginning, middle, and end. The jazz musician is a pure storyteller, extemporizing wordless tales charged with dramatic tension. The stories are funny, tragic, erotic, despondent, angry, playful, solemn, sacred, and defiant. They are delivered in a narrative idiom that, though it lacks words, is as rich in its range of plots and characters as any spoken language. Above all, *the jazz solo is experienced as story* by both musician and listener. A jazz solo leads its listeners on an imaginative journey. It creates a community of imaginations. The creation of that community — in which the only criterion for entry is the willingness to love — is the essential aim and magic of oral storytelling. Whether the storyteller is a parent sharing a bedtime tale with gleeful little children or an orator urging a nation to action, the magic is the same. Storytelling is an invitation to suspend ego, to share a momentary ride, to bleed or laugh a little together in a fragile zone of common meaning, not as automata acting or feeling in unison, but as unique men and women, each of whom will respond to the story differently. Each of whom will also recognize the telling universals that unite us all, not least of which is the simple act of faith required to listen with feeling.

Like all oralists, jazz musicians live, think, and create in the moment. They are extremely responsive to context and mood as they extemporize their tales, seeking maximum dramatic coherence in a unique story arc. Although they exploit harmonic and melodic tools such as scales, chords, chord changes, and formulaic song structures, for the jazz musician these tools are means to a greater end: the elaboration of a significant story — the creation of a community of imaginations united by sound. The greatest jazz soloists are unquestionably the greatest storytellers; they are the most visionary and coherent poets, those with the deepest knowledge of their inner voice.

Thus jazz expression is fundamentally oral, even when — especially when — singing voices are absent. It evolved as a language for a people without words, a people *denied* the vocabulary of words because of systematic disenfranchisement. In jazz, black America created a fluid idiomatic vocabulary with which to express the otherwise inexpressible. As jazz pianist Billy Taylor put it, "The men who created jazz had much to say. They were Negroes who found it impossible to voice their opinions verbally so they devised their own way of playing to get the freedom of expression they were otherwise denied."[10]

5 From Bessie to Billie

Blue History
Agamemnon
standing on deck
Iphigenia
prone at his feet
he raises a trumpet overhead
and blows

In Jerusalem
many years later
Pontius Pilate turns
to his prisoner asking:
" What is jazz?"

Thomas Aquinas
in the thirteenth century in Paris
secretly sings flatted
fifths at matins
that early Bird

Lenin
in his railway car in Switzerland
leans back after dinner
and listens to the soulful singing
of his emancipated
American porter

1959
in highest Lhasa, Tibet,
the Dalai Lama
escaping from the Chinese
has a vision of Billie Holiday
on her deathbed
under arrest

JAZZ IS THE VOICE DENIED WORDS. How then does it accommodate voices with words? In the early years of jazz, during the heyday of the classic blues singers — women like Ma Rainey, Bessie Smith, Trixie Smith, and Sippie Wallace — the language of jazz was the powerfully poetic language of the blues. This word-language was held in common by black Americans. Although traditional rural blues songs were often performed a cappella, or with the modest accompaniment of a guitar, harmonica, or jug, their simple yet potent poetic form was easily adapted to the sophisticated polyphonic settings that emerged in the urban north after World War I. Recorded and produced primarily for the black population, the lyrics on early "race records" were authentic expressions of popular African-American verbal idioms.

Bessie Smith's first recording, "Downhearted Blues," sold over 750,000 copies when it was released in 1923, making it the biggest-selling record in history at that time. One of those records was bought by a Jewish kid from Chicago named Milton "Mezz" Mezzrow. He was smart, sassy, and would become a lifelong jazz devotee. In his memoirs, co-written with Bernard Wolfe and titled *Really the Blues*, Mezzrow recalls the impact of Bessie Smith:

> What knocked me out most on these records was the slurring and division of words to fit the musical pattern, the way the words were put to work for the music. I tried to write them down

> because I figured the only way to dig Bessie's unique phrasing was to get the words down exactly as she sang them. It was something I had to do; there was a great secret buried in that woman's genius that I had to get. After every few words I'd stop the record to write the lyrics down, so my dad made a suggestion. Why didn't I ask my sister Helen to take down the words in shorthand? She was doing secretarial work and he figured it would be a cinch for her.
>
> If my sister had made a table-pad out of my best record or used my old horn for a garbage can she couldn't have made me hotter than she did that day. I've never been so steamed up, before or since. She was in a very proper and dicty mood, so she kept "correcting" Bessie's grammar, straightening out her words and putting them in "good" English until they sounded like some stuck-up jive from *McGuffy's Reader* instead of the real down-to-earth language of the blues ... I've never felt friendly to her to this day on account of how she laid her fancy high-school airs on the immortal Bessie Smith.[11]

It would not be long, however, before more imposing figures than Mezzrow's little sister would begin to lay their fancy airs on the language of Bessie Smith and her peers. As it became clear that many whites were willing to listen to honest and sensual black singers like Bessie Smith, white record-label owners felt it necessary to expunge the evil of the emotive and evocative honesty of the blues and replace it with something more wholesome and less dangerous. In other words, something white. So here is another paradox: that jazz singing truly became distinct from blues singing when it was forced to accommodate a foreign influence — predominantly white Tin Pan Alley tunesmiths and lyricists.[12]

Author Neil Leonard has compiled a highly instructive statistical analysis of the lyrical content of songs recorded by Bessie Smith between 1924 and 1928, and by Billie Holiday between 1936 and 1939. Leonard found that although fully two-thirds of Bessie Smith's songs were marked by a cynical outlook or mistrust of human nature, only 10 per cent of Billie Holiday's recorded repertoire acknowledged the dark side of human feeling. Further, 76 per cent of Bessie Smith's songs mentioned infidelity or mistreatment, whereas only 17 per cent of Lady

Day's songs did so. Most tellingly, however, 38 per cent of Bessie Smith's songs proposed action as a solution to unhappiness compared to only 6 per cent of Billie Holiday's.

Elements of lyrics that increased after 1928 represented, not surprisingly, the sort of romantic idealism that characterized Tin Pan Alley. Not one of Bessie Smith's songs proposed love as an ideal state, whereas fully 46 per cent of Billie's songs did so. Actual or possible happiness was described in only 6 per cent of Bessie's songs but in half of Billie's. Finally, 20 per cent of Billie's songs proposed dreams as a solution to unhappiness, but not a single song recorded by Bessie Smith did so.

If Billie Holiday and Bessie Smith had been very different kinds of women, perhaps this comparison would be less notable. But as different as they were in some respects, in many others, notably their poor taste in men, their fiery tempers and fierce dignity, their determination to succeed, their self-destructiveness, the passion with which they sang, and the brutality of the racist world they lived in, Bessie Smith and Billie Holiday had a great deal in common. So why did Bessie employ lyrics of gut-wrenching intensity while Billie sang banal ditties? The answer is simple. Bessie Smith had access to the language of the blues. Billie Holiday did not. Billie Holiday was forced to distance herself from the lyrics and songs she had grown up listening to, namely those of Bessie Smith, and she was instead pushed by her record labels toward the dreamy, white-bread world of Tin Pan Alley romance. Leonard sums up his findings this way:

> Before 1928 jazz lyrics reflected the life of the Negro subculture. Usually there were frank statements of fundamental human problems and feelings, uninhibited utterances of joy, humor, love, sensuality, anger, sorrow, pain. They found expression in simple salty language, concrete figures of speech and strong rhythms. Such lyrics allowed jazz singers to improvise easily and to evoke deep feelings in some listeners. But after 1928 jazz lyrics exemplified the traditional inclination of Americans to divorce music from practical affairs.[13]

The divorcing of music from practical affairs was yet another attack on the African heritage of functional creative expression. The usurping of idiomatic language by elevated flowery language ruptured the close relationship between speech and song that was also part of that heritage. Although black jazz singers were largely dispossessed of their indigenous poetic language by the 30s, this fact did not stop them from charging the language they did have with meaning. The result of this dispossession was widespread resistance in the form of stylistic evasions from these new linguistic shackles.

In the late 20s and 30s, scat singing and deliberately altered or garbled language were among the most widely used means of escape. Louis Armstrong and Cab Calloway were adepts of these evasive methods. Double entendre and subtle satiric hints were also part of the black jazz singer's repertoire in trying to escape the shallow lyrics and reclaim a legitimate and relevant poetic voice. These latter tactics were not difficult to master because they were already familiar elements of the black tradition of communication through buried meanings.

As the classic blues singers gradually went out of fashion by the early 30s, their place was taken in the popular ear by a new kind of singer: the big band vocalists. Eastern big bands like those of Fletcher Henderson and Duke Ellington continued to use blues lyrics in their early music, but once Bing Crosby achieved national acclaim in 1927 with the Paul Whiteman Orchestra, record companies became keen to cash in on the commercial appeal of big band crooners. So as the big bands grew in popularity, the demand for black singers to sing white show tunes increased. It was standard practice throughout the swing era to have a female singer in every big band, and often a male voice too. Jazz musicians called them "canaries." The term is apt, as it brings to mind a pretty bird chirping, wordlessly. The tepid love songs the big band singers were given to sing handcuffed much of their power. Where was the emotional intensity, the poetic truth, the transcendent impulse, in a song like Jerome Kern and Dorothy Fields's much-loved "A Fine Romance"?

A fine romance, with no kisses!
A fine romance, my friend, this is!
We should be like a couple of hot tomatoes,
But you're as cold as yesterday's mashed potatoes.

A fine romance! My good fellow!
You take romance, I'll take Jell-O!
You're calmer than the seals in the Arctic Ocean.
At least they flap their fins to express emotion[14]

Some Tin Pan Alley songs stand up better: "Stormy Weather," "All of Me," "Just Friends," "Georgia on My Mind," to name a few. Yet even those songs, which have tolerably sensible lyrics, not overloaded with references to seals or Jell-O, are still astonishingly narrow in tone and subject. Idealized romantic love was virtually the only subject canaries could sing about. With the poetry of the blues exiled from the mainstream, the words and images foisted on singers were of the shallowest variety. As a result, jazz vocalists of the time often chose to concentrate more on *how* they sang their lyrics rather than on their literal meaning.

Remarkably, the greatest jazz singer of them all, Billie Holiday, rejected this means of escape. Instead, her method was to devote herself with such fervour to the vapid lyrics that even the tritest of songs was jolted with the electric force of her poetic spirit. She unflinchingly confronted the triviality of her lyrics, extracting from them nuances and depths nobody had imagined were present. In so doing, she recreated each song in her own image. Unlike most jazz standards, which have been sung by generations of singers, many of the songs Billie Holiday made famous remain almost untouched today, such is the shadow she cast.

Yet Billie was only human. She could not create something out of nothing. She worked with what she had and accomplished extraordinary things, but she was nonetheless locked within a carefully tended Victorian garden of poetry. Although in her career she sang no more than a handful of songs with lyrics equal to her interpretive capacity, we do have a few indications of what might have been. One is a song Lady Day first sang in 1937:

Strange Fruit

Southern trees
bear a strange fruit
blood on the leaves
blood at the root

Black bodies swinging
in the southern breeze
strange fruit hanging
from the poplar trees

pastoral scene
of the gallant south
the bulging eyes
the twisted mouth
scent of magnolia
sweet and fresh
then the sudden smell
of burning flesh

here is a fruit
for the prole to pluck
for the rain to gather
for the wind to suck
for the sun to rot
for the tree to drop
here is a strange
and bitter
crop[15]

Billie Holiday remarked on “Strange Fruit” in her as-told-to autobiography, *Lady Sings the Blues*:

> It was during my stint at Café Society that a song was born which became my personal protest — “Strange Fruit.” The germ of the song was in a poem by Lewis Allen. When he showed me that poem, I dug it right off. It seemed to spell out all the things that had killed Pop.[16]

The only two songs Billie Holiday recorded that she wrote herself, “Don’t Explain” and “God Bless the Child,” allow us a glimpse of her own chosen language. Both songs speak of life with a frankness and perspicacity far outstripping the sentimental ballads that made up the bulk of her repertoire. “God Bless the Child” is a simple yet moving lament, the song of a woman who's seen it all but remains an innocent at heart:

Them's that's got shall get
Them that's not shall lose
so the Bible says
and it still is news
Mama may have
Papa may have
but God bless the child
that's got his own
that's got his own[17]

On July 17, 1959, as she lay trembling in hospital on her deathbed, America's greatest singer was arrested by the New York Police Department and charged with possession of heroin. She had given the world all that was in her power to give.

6 Lush Life

In Pittsburgh one night in the mid-30s, between sets with his orchestra, Duke Ellington was approached at the piano by a shy, bespectacled young man. Duke was already a legend by this time, but ever the gentleman, he received his young admirer warmly. The local youth — a teenager — asked if he could play Duke a song he'd written. Duke allowed he could. So Billy Strayhorn sat down and played. When the song was over, Duke was silent, his face betraying little but his eyes twinkling with delight. "Call me when you get to New York," he then said to the young man. And a few years later — in 1938 — Billy Strayhorn did call Duke Ellington. From that day forward, he became Duke's lifelong friend and musical collaborator. Strayhorn even wrote Duke Ellington's signature tune, "Take the A Train," along with countless other classics. But it was that first song, the tune he played for Duke that night back in Pittsburgh, that remains Strayhorn's most enduring achievement. The song was "Lush Life":

I used to go to all those very gay places
those come what may places
where one relaxes on the axis of the wheel of life
to get the feel of life
from jazz and cocktails

The girls I knew had sad and sullen gray faces
with distingué traces
that used to be there you could see where they'd been washed away
by too many through the day
twelve o'clocktails

Then you came along
with your siren song
to tempt me to madness
I thought for a while
that your poignant smile
was tinged with the sadness
of a great love for me
Ah yes, I was wrong
Again, I was wrong

Life is lonely
again and only last year
everything seemed so sure
now life is awful
again a troughful of hearts
would only be a bore

A week in Paris
would ease the bite of it
all I care is to smile
in spite of it

I'll forget you
I will while yet you are still
burning inside my brain
romance is mush
stifling those who strive
I'll live a lush life
in some small dive
and there I'll be
while I rot with the rest
of those whose lives are lonely too[18]

Why is Billy Strayhorn's "Lush Life" a perfect — perhaps the only perfect — jazz song? Strayhorn set out to translate his life experience — and his dreams — into what was essentially a foreign language. Strayhorn successfully translated the oral sophistication embodied in his musical composition into a word-language that expressed an equally articulate literate intelligence. No jazz composer had ever before united oral and literate idioms with such organic and beautiful results. In so doing, he achieved a degree of poetic sophistication that dwarfed the accomplishments of even the most subtle of Tin Pan Alley tunesmiths. As both lyricist and composer, Strayhorn not only took possession of a vocabulary typically denied black lyricists, but succeeded in enriching it with a daringly sympathetic musicality. Words and music are utterly intertwined in "Lush Life," with the cognitive meaning of every word sensually and emotionally enhanced by its sensitive melodic treatment. "Lush Life" departs confidently from the standard formulas that dominated the songwriting of the day. Its sophisticated psychology stands in gleaming contrast to the essential banality of most others of its era. The song's narrator speaks with a directness and a humility that is as unpretentious and effective as that of the blues singer. In these lyrics, Strayhorn returns the singer to real life, to the community, abandoning phony idealism and explicitly rejecting romance. Even when Strayhorn uses complex words or images, like *distingué* or *troughful*, they seem to follow naturally from the demands of the speaker and his tone; it's as if he were there before you, and these were the words he spontaneously chose in conversation. The tension between the narrator's jaded passivity and his awareness of his remaining potential is allowed to build slowly, naturally, without artifice or formality. When the song ends, we feel we have genuinely met someone, have been given access to his true feelings, have heard his secret voice.

Even in its written form "Lush Life" is extraordinarily singable. Its music jumps off the page in a way the cliché-ridden fluff of "A Fine Romance" could never do. It is almost impossible to read its lyrics out loud without one's voice slipping into a musical lilt. (In his *Treatise on Meter*, Ezra Pound wrote, "... we will never recover the art of *writing to be sung* until we begin to pay some attention to the sequence, or scale, of vowels in the line, and of the vowels terminating the group of lines in a series."[19]) Anchored by its exquisite vowel scales, the lyrics of "Lush

Life" swing unceasingly: "I'll forget you / I will while yet you are still / burning inside my brain."

The song's ambition is startling and the ease with which its effects are achieved is stunning. But why is it the only perfect jazz song? Because unlike almost any other song sung by jazz singers until the 60s (when an era of experimentation was ushered in by the likes of Oscar Brown Jr. and Nina Simone), "Lush Life" was created by a brilliant jazz composer in full possession of a mature, poetic word-language, with a deep story to tell.

Some jazz historians report the origin of "Lush Life" differently, suggesting Strayhorn played another song for Duke that night in Pittsburgh; that "Lush Life" was instead written after Strayhorn arrived in New York. On the other hand, maybe — as legend has it — Strayhorn really did write "Lush Life" at the age of sixteen, foreshadowing the tenor of his own life as a gay black man travelling the world, creating wonderful music, ducking publicity, and standing knowingly in Duke Ellington's long shadow. The facts are irrelevant. Strayhorn's legacy is his music and his songs.

7 Scat Singing

> I have witnessed congregations moved to ecstasy by the rhythmic intoning of sheer incoherencies.
>
> — JAMES WELDON JOHNSON, *God's Trombones*

JAZZ MUSIC GAVE BLACK AMERICA AN IDIOM with which to push the envelope of public language. But when black America pushed, white America pushed back, working to limit the authenticity, energy, and potency of black oral expression. Because jazz vocalists in the 30s were generally restricted to singing songs whose lyrics had little intrinsic poetic value to the black community, they found other ways to make their public voices as meaningful as possible. In scat singing, black oralists found a means of escape, a playful arena where their improvisatory urges could be given free rein and they could explode the restrictive limitations of banal lyrics. Louis Armstrong did so on his historic 1926 recording, "Heebie Jeebies":

Yes, ma'am, poppa's got the heebie jeebies bad, ay
Eef, gaff, mmmff, dee-bo, duh-deedle-la bahm,
Rip-bip-ee-doo-dee-doot, doo
Roo-dee-doot duh-dee-dut-duh-dut,
Skeep, skam, skee-bo-de-dah-de-dat, doop-dum-dee,

Frantic rhythm, so come on down, do that dance,
They call the heebie jeebies dance, sweet mammo,
poppa's got to do the heebie jeebies dance[20]

Legend has it that Armstrong's fanciful riffing on "Heebie Jeebies," which almost overnight set off a popular scat-singing craze, came as a result of Pops dropping his sheet music in mid-verse. He carried on, scattering nonsense as he went, and the resulting recording changed jazz history.

Louis Armstrong's weird riffs were christened *scat*, which can be defined as the art of singing nonsense syllables during vocal improvisations in a jazz setting. Although it is reasonable and accurate to link scat singing with African vocal traditions, the oft-referenced interpretation of that relationship — specifically the idea that scat is a retention of African words — is way off the mark. Every jazz singer develops his or her own distinct vocabulary of scat sounds of which few — if any — phonemes can legitimately be traced to retained Hausa or Ibo or Bantu words. The real story is simpler and deeper.

Scat singing has its origins in the demands of playing music and in particular of playing jazz music. All musicians, when they discuss music, sing to each other. In singing, they try to replicate the musical styles and sonorities they use when they play. This practice holds true for cellists, bagpipers, and tabla players. And so it is with jazz musicians. Long before Louis Armstrong's recording, when Sidney Bechet taught his bandmates the melody of a new tune for a dance at Lake Pontchartrain, or when Freddy Keppard told his brother about a riff Buddy Bolden had played that afternoon, these musicians sang to each other wordlessly using jazz phrasing. In other words, they were scat singing. It might be accurate to say that before "Heebie Jeebies," nobody scatted in public as a part of a performance. But even this contention is questionable. Danny Barker thought scatting went back long before "Heebie Jeebies":

> Scat singing, Louis Armstrong made it popular, but people had been doing it all the time. But Louis Armstrong made it nationwide popular with the "Heebie Jeebies." During the minstrel days, musicians did scat singing, with a scat dance, you know. They did a thing a sofus-gofus-goofus-goofus-gofus-geefus, you

> know, that kind of thing, with the eyeballs and all that business. That was always to provoke laughs, you know. All of a sudden you're speaking something nobody can understand but you, and you're doing it with a know-how.[21]

With its emphasis on rhythm and sound rather than cognitive meaning, scat can more reasonably be traced to showbiz and musician-speak than to a misremembered African linguistic heritage. Yet scat must also be recognized as a legacy of the same African oral heritage that informed jazz as a whole. All too familiar with the intricacies of coded communication, both audiences and performers easily grasped and fully embraced the subtle humour and playful commentaries conveyed in nonsense singing.

Although scat can be meaningful to a certain degree in an aphasic or coded sense, it is nonetheless an immature language that can never attain the level of significance afforded by a word-language, or by a fully developed non-semantic communicative idiom such as jazz. Several singers, among them Jimmy Rushing and Billie Holiday, refused to have anything to do with scat singing. Perhaps they saw scat as offensively facile, considering their own efforts as artists and individuals to overcome linguistic restrictions. Others, however, particularly in the 30s and early 40s, saw scat as a useful gimmick and developed their own scat dialects, which became fashionable among young fans. Two of the most prominent of these were Cab Calloway and Leo Watson.

Calloway's most famous scat syllables are "hi-de-hi-de-hi-de-hi ho-de-ho-de-ho-de-hooo," which he wailed with bellow-like lungs and enormous exuberance. He also elaborated an entire jive dialect, which, while great for record sales and his fey image, was not always the same as that spoken on the street. Danny Barker had this to say about his bandleader's vocalizing:

> It didn't matter whether we understood all those different words because we had the melodies. And after a while you just accepted it. And it was a routine, it was scatting that had the form of a song, so you knew how the song was supposed to end if you're a musician. You know what the release is, the middle part, if they had one, and you went along with that. And it was nonsense so you

> didn't take too much — it was great for him to project that to the audience, but the musicians, they went along with it.[22]

In 1933, Cab Calloway and his orchestra recorded a ditty called "The Scat Song" for RCA. The uptempo piece begins with a bit of romping stride piano by Bennie Payne. Almost instantly, Calloway enters with a sizzling scat phrase that goes something like "Geeg-li-a-leep-vzap-vzap-la-de-dap-skee-dee-bee-dee-lope-dope-doby ..."

One of the musicians then interrupts him, calling: "Say, what 'cha doin' boy?"

Cab replies: "Oh, man, I'm just scattin' and goin' right on the town, saxy mama."

Then comes the first verse. Cab sings two lines: "When your sweety tells you, /everything'll be o.k." Here, instead of the concluding two-line scat riff we are led to expect, a two-bar trumpet break follows, in which the trumpet player imitates scat singing on his horn.

The second verse continues: "Don't you give a hang what words you use at anytime, / just use this silly language without any reason or rhyme." This time an alto sax takes the two-bar break in place of Cab's scat.

Finally, the third verse runs: "When you thank the preacher / There's only one thing to say." Here the two-bar solo break is taken by the entire orchestra in an arranged ensemble passage that sounds like "oo-wa oo-wa oo-wa oo-wa oop-de dab-a-dab-dee-doh."

"The Scat Song"'s unique form allows us to easily compare its instrumental solo breaks with Cab's scat singing. Calloway's opening statement swaggers with madcap confidence. The hi-de-ho man is in full control of his loopy vocabulary, and here he babbles magnificently. The same cannot be said for the instrumentalists who take the solo breaks. Interestingly, we have an alternative take of "The Scat Song," and in both versions, they display the same lack of finesse and uncertainty in their instrumental solo breaks. This is especially odd because the musicians in Calloway's band were all excellent players with complete command of their musical idiom. In other songs, as plenty of recordings demonstrate, these same players (likely Doc Cheatham on trumpet and Eddie Barefield on alto) attack solo breaks with plenty of verve and dexterity. Why should these particular breaks have caused them so much difficulty? Why do they sound like amateurs on "The Scat Song"?

The answer lies in the title of the song and in the instructions Calloway appears to have given his musicians to imitate scat singing on their horns. The unusual substitution of instrumental breaks where vocal ones logically ought to be suggests that Cab must have directed his soloists to take his place as scatters during the breaks. The shoddy results confirm it. Had Cab understood the relationship of scat singing to jazz as a whole, he would have understood that none of his musicians could possibly do what he had asked.

The difficulty Calloway's musicians faced in these solo breaks, and which caused them to lose their usually unimpeachable musical cool, was that the vocabulary of jazz instrumental expression had, in a mere thirty years, developed an internal coherence and expressive capacity of far greater depth than the wordless vocalizing of scat could ever hope to attain. When the two soloists tried to imitate scat, they were confronted and confused by a collision of two aesthetic purposes. The musicians had apprenticed for years to learn how to communicate succinctly and purposefully in a wordless language, and their endeavours were so successful that each note they played was part of a common vocabulary, fluently understood by other jazz musicians and by a well-attuned community of listeners. *Their language did not permit itself to be made meaningless.* The first principle of jazz expression is you must mean what you say. The aim of each solo was to tell a story in the moment, articulating the immediacy of experience as meaningfully as possible. But scat is essentially meaningless. So when asked to imitate its empty vocables, these same musicians found it musically, physically, and emotionally impossible.

In the mid-40s, another vocalist rose to prominence with a scatter-brained scat style that outdid even Calloway's. His name was Leo Watson. Watson's wacky songs mixed words and nonsense syllables in equal measure. Whereas most scat singers maintained a clear distinction between a song's legitimate lyrics and the improvised wordless solos elaborated over the song's chord changes, Watson slipped in and out of scat phonemes without hesitation. After one listens to his recordings for a while, even real words begin to sound invented as a result of his constant playful distortions of their sound. He often eschewed anything resembling syllabic phonemes, and simply wailed and swooped in some very peculiar arabesques.

Leo Watson was born in Kansas City in 1898. He had begun touring as a solo singer in the 1920s, and when Louis Armstrong legitimized scat, Leo Watson was one of the first and freshest to follow his lead. Watson's group, The Spirits of Rhythm, was an on-again-off-again act through the 30s and 40s. In 1939, the group recorded "It's the Tune That Counts," which might be considered Watson's musical manifesto:

It makes no difference what you sing
a little opera, a little swing,
make it sweet, make it bounce
tiddly-hoy-hoy-hoy it's the tune that counts[23]

Subsequent lyrics veer off into a frenzied mix of nonsense lyrics and scat riffs that defies transcription. Watson twists words inside out, upside down, and sideways before climaxing on his final, flipped-out note. Despite what his song proclaims, it is ultimately neither the lyrics nor the tune that counts with Leo Watson. It is simply the unchained vocal angel in full lunatic flight. As his old cohort and comrade in scat, Slim Gaillard, puts it: "He was original. Everybody in Hollywood used to come in and listen to him. And they'd follow everything he said, because he could sing about anything. He'd start singing about the walls, the rug, tables, ashtray, he'd just sing. Yes, I guess he was up in the skies somewhere."[24]

So scat represents both the momentary liberation of an oral people from its oppressor's dictionary and a symptom of the continuing intensity of that oppression. And scat can also be seen as a potent manifestation of a specific oral tradition, that of unintelligible poetry, as described by ethnopoetic visionary Jerome Rothenberg: "Such special languages — meaningless and/or mysterious — are a small but nearly universal part of 'primitive-archaic' poetry. They may involve 1) purely invented meaningless sounds; 2) distortion of ordinary words and syntax; 3) ancient words emptied of their long since forgotten meanings; 4) words borrowed from other languages and likewise emptied."[25]

8 Eddie Jefferson

As early as 1938, inspired by Leo Watson's inventiveness, a young tap dancer named Eddie Jefferson began to amuse himself — and his jazz musician friends — by putting words to famous recorded jazz solos. Jefferson and his dance partner Irv Taylor incorporated the gimmick into their stage act, mimicking solos by tenor players like Lester Young or Chu Berry. A couple of years later, as bebop gathered steam, Jefferson, who had by then split up with Taylor, sang solos by Dizzy and Bird, dexterously duplicating their rapid riffing and adding playful lyrics. In 1950, Jefferson recorded two songs, "I Cover the Waterfront" and "Parker's Mood," but the records went more or less unnoticed. He kept singing, performing his songs in nightclubs, including Cincinnati's The Cotton Club, where he served up his idiosyncratic vocals to appreciative audiences. Among the solos Jefferson sang there was "Moody's Mood" (based on "I'm in the Mood For Love"), a tune released in 1952 by saxman James Moody. It was a huge surprise to Jefferson when a recording featuring his lyrics to "Moody's Mood" was a smash hit in 1953. It was even voted R & B song of the year by *Downbeat Magazine*. Jefferson's surprise was particularly profound because he had never recorded the song. The hit record was by a singer named King Pleasure, a former bartender at The Cotton Club in Cincinnati. King Pleasure had copped Jefferson's lyrics word for word and thus taken credit not only for writing them, but for pioneering a new singing style that would soon be termed *vocalese.*

In some jazz histories King Pleasure remains credited as the originator of vocalese, but several accounts make it clear that he simply ripped off Eddie Jefferson's concept and lyrical content. Though dishonest, King Pleasure nonetheless managed to establish vocalese as a popular style, which allowed Jefferson to build an erratic yet significant career. And though jazz histories tend to slight his abilities and importance, to my ear Eddie Jefferson is hands down the greatest vocalese lyricist and singer, if only for his having produced *Letter from Home,* the most exciting, beautiful, and soulful vocalese album ever made.

Jefferson's early recordings from the 50s sound immature, made before the one-time dancer had mastered his singing voice. And on later recordings, made during the 70s after Jefferson had been rediscovered by altoist Richie Cole, the singer's voice is tired and worn. On those later albums, the bloom of youth is clearly gone. But between these two bookends, there is one album in particular, *Letter from Home,* recorded in 1961 for Riverside, that catches Eddie Jefferson in absolutely perfect form. With impeccably swinging big band arrangements by Ernie Wilkins and the improvisational contributions of James Moody, Johnny Griffin, and Clark Terry among others, *Letter from Home* achieves a unity of purpose, execution, and style that sets it apart from all other vocalese records, including the much-heralded Lambert, Hendricks, and Ross LPs. Jefferson engages his listeners in each lyrical vignette as much by his love of life as by his dazzling vocal acrobatics and unusual lyrics. In "A Night in Tunisia," Jefferson designed a jazz fairy tale around Dizzy's famous solo. As the band reaches the climax of its charge toward that wondrously designed solo break, it catapults Eddie Jefferson into flight, and the singer takes off, riding a propulsive groove on a surreal poetic arc.

Jefferson was never a popular performer. He spent most of his career in relative obscurity, from which he only began to emerge in the late 70s. His life ended tragically, however, when he was fatally shot outside a Detroit nightclub by an apparent stranger in 1979. The murderer was apprehended and tried but released on a technicality.

Eddie Jefferson's lyrics and the style in which he delivered them are significant because they signify a reintegration of language with music, with the body. Jefferson's songs were the expression of an individual world view, articulated neither in the wordless idiom of jazz instrumentalists, nor in the artificial vocabulary of the standard jazz song repertoire, nor still in wordless scatting, but in an unfettered declarative voice. That Jefferson's range as a lyricist is ultimately modest in scope does not undermine the essential power of his achievement. With Jefferson, it is the complete package that matters.

Despite vocalese's potential to provide black singers with access to their own uncensored idiomatic language, several factors conspired to limit the influence of Jefferson's innovations. The first is technical, arising from the unique demands placed on the vocalese singer. Simply put, vocalese is an extremely difficult singing style to master, requiring vocalists to move with the speed and dexterity of instrumentalists. Second, although vocalese invites each singer/composer to explore his or her personal vocabulary and poetic imagination, that exploration is arguably incompatible with the restrictive melodic requirements of vocalese. In other words, putting highly charged words to highly charged prerecorded melodies necessitates a difficult balancing act, one only rarely managed successfully in the jazz tradition. Perhaps most significant of all was the increasing gulf between jazz and black pop music, a gulf that placed the musical sophistication of *Letter from Home* on a diverging trajectory from that of a new generation of R & B stars such as Smokey Robinson, Stevie Wonder, and James Brown, and their fans. As a result, Eddie Jefferson's contribution remains in a sense unexploited. Despite its ability to expand the lyrical range of black poetry in music, vocalese ultimately proved to be an exciting and challenging dead end in black America's search for a fully functional poetic word-language.

9 Slang and Jive

SLANG IS A MANIFESTATION of human poetic capacity in everyday speech. Jazz slang — the multitude of words, phrases, argots, and nicknames invented and employed by jazz musicians and their audiences — has always existed in relation to the delineation of the form, subject matter, and vocabulary of African-American public speech by the infrastructure of American racism. The evolution of jazz slang is yet another escape into coded meaning, another expression of the African oral heritage, and another step toward the full emancipation of meaning and feeling in a complete and mature public language.

Interestingly, slang — and the need to create coded idioms — was a vital part of the African oral heritage even before its arrival in America. Although the breadth and scope of slang usage was vastly enhanced in the deprived communicative circumstances of slavery, slang itself is far older than the Middle Crossing.

Moreover, the poetic principle underlying slang is much deeper than is generally understood. Slang has its origins in sympathetic magic. Charms and spells are traditionally vital components of oral cultures, in which the evocation of unseen essences in language and the creation of coded idioms accessible to privileged initiates is seen as a key to a collective survival. Thus the African conception of language included and still includes a belief in the magical power of poetic metaphor and the ability of indirection to evoke transformative essences. This same faith in language as sympathetic magic can be found throughout the pre-literate world among the Inuit, Navajo, Maori, and many other cultures. Of course, the same belief is also found at the heart of several of the world's major religions, including Christianity, Judaism, Hinduism, and Islam. "In the beginning was the word" is an ancient and near-universal refrain.

Jazz music is itself a slang language. It is a form of African-American slang. It seeks to evoke the imperceptible, essential qualities of existence in metaphor. Not all music has this aim. European compositional traditions, for example, are far less referential than jazz. Although one can point to individual works such as Vivaldi's *The Four Seasons*, Holst's *The Planets*, and Debussy's *Prélude à l'après-midi d'un faune*, the representation of experience was only rarely the explicit or implicit aim of European composers. Jazz recordings, on the other hand, are bursting with poetic references intelligible to the black listener who had been trained to infer the maximum possible information from the most veiled indications. Here is Duke Ellington, discussing his early days as a composer and bandleader, speaking about the representation of reality in music:

> Bubber and Tricky were the first to get really wide recognition for the plunger thing. They had such beautiful teamwork together. Everything they played represented a mood, a person, a picture. As a matter of fact, everything we used to do in the old days had a picture. We'd be riding along and see a name on a sign. We used to spend a lot of time up in New England, around Boston, and we'd see this sign — LEWANDO CLEANERS — and every time we saw it we'd start singing:
>
> "Oh, Lee-wan-do!"
>
> Out of that came East St. Louis Toodle-oo. Probably it would have been better if we had called it Lewando and got some advertising money for it. Everything was like that then. The guys would be walking up Broadway after work and see this old man coming down the street, and there was the beginning of Old Man Blues. Everything had a picture or was descriptive of something. Always.[26]

Jazz is the creative commentary of a people denied access to a fully functional word-language and its essence is metaphor. It is a slang dialect, a playful poetic patois of essentials. Neil Leonard explains that "the jazz initiand . . . was particularly sensitive to indirect and buried meanings — significances at the edge of conventional articulation and comprehension. In exploring these meanings, jazzmen regressed into mental states with deep-structured rules of associational logic and resorted to ritual and myth, the handmaidens of logic and the sacred."[27]

The improvisatory and metaphor-making skills jazz musicians possessed led them to engage in lively and humorous wordplay. And that wordplay — required to capture the essence of the jazz identity, the jazz vision, the jazz soul, that constantly changing slang idiom of the jazz musician — proved a key source of poetic language for all of America. In fact, jazz is one of the richest sources of popular American slang. Many terms first gained currency among black musicians and entertainers and then were adopted by the larger black community. From there, they moved into the vocabulary of white trendsetters who latched onto black slang terms both because of their linguistic potency and their risqué edge. The terms then went mainstream, adopted into popular American speech, where many of them remain firmly embedded today. *Cool* for example, began as a jazz term denoting a musical approach, but the word has since mushroomed into a concept, a lifestyle, a cultural imperative, a marketing motherlode, a global style. The potency of cool is directly tied to the ability to convey a wealth of meanings by an extensive vocabulary of coded idioms, most of which are non-verbal; because attitude is not what you say — it's who you are, how you carry yourself, the look in your eyes, your shoes, clothes, walk. In the U.S. today, the acting out of the coded idiom of cool encompasses almost every aspect of adolescent life.

The first important transfer of slang from the jazz world to mainstream America was the word jazz itself. Originally a verb spelled "jass," the word was a euphemism for sexual intercourse, possibly derived from *jism*. Jazz music was so named because of the close relationship between the music and sex. Not only did the two often exist in physical proximity (jazz music was at home in the brothels of New Orleans), but the seductive nature of the music itself (which was popular at dances) also contributed to the consolidation of the word's meaning. When the word was adopted into the popular vocabulary in the years that followed, its sexual overtones were downplayed, yet they remained as an undertone in what would prove to be a liberal and highly sexualized era, The Jazz Age.

"Jazz it up" and "jazzy" have since become common expressions in American speech. And over the years, many other words have made the leap, including such essential definitions of popular culture as *funky*, *square*, and *hip*. Yet other expressions derived from jazz are *blow your top*, *pay your dues*, *chick*, *honkytonk*, *soul*, *swing* (another lifestyle), and *rock 'n' roll*, which was used in jazz circles to describe the erotic rhythms of black music long before it was applied in the mid-50s to a raunchy electrified baby of country music and blues. A cursory examination of a dictionary of American slang will turn up countless examples of well-known words and sayings coined by jazz musicians. Many commonly used slang superlatives, words like *wild*, *crazy*, *hot*, and *freaky*, derive from the need for black musicians to find new ways of describing the emotional heights reached in their playing.

Jazz nicknames are often metaphoric symbols of a person's inner qualities, character, or stature in the community. "Pops" was so called because Louis Armstrong enjoyed the reputation as a father figure to an entire generation of jazzmen. "Dizzy" was so named because of John Birks Gillespie's unpredictable antics and proclivity for clowning on and off stage. "Lucky" Millinder, "Hot Lips" Page, "Slow Drag" Pavageau, Kenny "Klook" Clark, "Bunny" Berrigan, and a host of others got their names because of the comic wit of a bandmate. As products of an oral culture, jazz icons are nearly all verbal or musical. Nicknames are among the most important of them. The insight, humour, and creativity with which they are chosen embody perfectly the aims of the jazz spirit. Many of the same principles apply today to rap artists, although the aggressive connotations of many contemporary MC names reflect the widespread violence afflicting black communities rather than the optimism that characterized jazz slang.

Mezz Mezzrow wonderfully describes that optimism — and its impact on language:

> I heard the jive language in its early stages, when I was hanging around the South Side in Chicago. It was the first furious babbling of a people who suddenly woke up to find their death sentence

> had been revoked, or at least postponed; and they were stunned and dazzled at first, hardly able to believe it. Then came the full exuberant waking up, the full realization that the bossman, or at least the peckerwood kind with a bullwhip in his hand, was gone. The music got wilder and wilder. The excited rush of talk on streetcorners, and in poolrooms and ginmills, swelled up to a torrent.[28]

The talk swelled up until it became ... jive. Jive is slang on speed. Slang souped up to the point where slang phrases outnumber "real" words, where entirely new syntaxes emerge, where playing with rhythm and rhyme becomes the very goal of speech. Jive is conversation as poetry. Jive is jazz. Mezzrow understood this perfectly:

> Jive isn't just a reflection of a primitive state. Not by a long shot. The Negro doesn't add action metaphors to abstractions, put movement into static phrases, throw warmth into frozen logical categories, just because he can't understand them any other way. That's open to question. What is sure is he's got too much poetry and rhythmic feeling in him, still alive and kicking, to be expressed in the bookish accents of educated white speech. He's got to pep up that bedraggled lingo to hold his interest and give vent to his emotions.[29]

Yet despite its vitality, jive was still slang, still a coded idiom. It was not a language given to all but earned by the few. Jive was a playful improvisatory idiom in which metaphor ruled and slick wit and verbal style were valued above all. One that could only be learned by listening — and by practising. But the only way to practise jive was to participate in conversations, to learn in the moment, to stumble and trip until you got it right. There were no jive scales to practise. There was only the naked ear, the rhythms of the body, the flow of imagination.

Like scat singing, jive was exploited as a commercial gimmick. Again Cab Calloway was at the forefront of the commercializing of jive, even publishing *Mr. Hepster's (Not Webster's) Jive Dictionary*, a compendium of jive talk for the uninitiated. His was not the only such book. Several others were available in the early 50s, including *The Jives of Dr. Hepcat*, written by an Austin, Texas-based DJ of the same name.

Black DJs were essential to the evolution of jive, spinning their unique patter between songs for audiences across America. The first of the over-the-top jive-talking black DJs was New Orleans's Dr. Daddy-O, whose *Jivin with Jax* show on WWEZ premiered in 1949 after its host finally managed to overcome the resistance of the white broadcast establishment to the idea of a black disc jockey. Throughout the 50s and 60s the best black DJs were enormously popular local celebrities. Their energetic jiving commentaries are also a significant precursor of rap, although that influence would only come to fruition once it had been fully absorbed elsewhere, by Jamaica's original dub MCs in the 60s and early 70s. The playful jive commentaries or *toasts* of Jamaican DJs, dubbed live over R & B-tinged instrumental mixes and played at ear-shattering volumes, were the immediate catalyst for the development of rap, after Jamaican block-party king Kool Herc imported them to the South Bronx in the mid-70s. A fuse lit in the tinderbox of black poetic orality.

10 A Love Supreme

On December 9, 1964, saxophonist John Coltrane led his band into Rudy Van Gelder's Hackensack, New Jersey, studio to record his thirteenth album for Impulse Records. Along with the familiar members of Coltrane's quartet — drummer Elvin Jones, pianist McCoy Tyner, and bassist Jimmy Garrison — saxophonist Archie Shepp and bassist Art Davis were also present. Bob Thiele was there too. He had produced most of Coltrane's recordings for Impulse and was familiar with his repertoire. But that day he would hear something different. Coltrane and his band would record music that had only recently been conceived in deepest meditation, music that sought explicitly to articulate and embody an ecstatic mysticism, music that would ultimately prove a threshold in Coltrane's extraordinary creative journey. The band would record four tracks: "Acknowledgement," "Resolution," "Pursuance," and "Psalm." Collectively, they constitute a suite titled *A Love Supreme*.

Why was it called *A Love Supreme*?

In the fall of 1964, Coltrane spent many long hours reading portions of works such as the Bhagavad-Gita and Kabbalistic texts. He would often meditate deep into the night, and his marathon saxophone studies had long since adopted a devotional tone, lasting endless hours without regard for external distractions. (Once he played ceaselessly for two weeks with his metal mouthpiece vibrating shrilly against his raw gums as he waited for new dentures.) It was clear to all who were close to him — as it soon would be to his growing legion of fans — that Coltrane was experiencing a spiritual rebirth. *A Love Supreme* was the herald of that renaissance. Coltrane was taking after his grandfathers, both of whom had been ministers. Like them, he had become a man of the cloth, although his was a pantheistic fabric.

A Love Supreme is now one of the most revered albums in the history of jazz, listened to by innumerable music lovers, which is what makes musicologist Lewis Porter's discovery all the more remarkable. In the mid-80s, Porter grasped a truth that had gone undetected by countless others. He was listening to the LP for the umpteenth time, casually reading over the devotional poem Coltrane had written and had printed inside the album jacket, when he had a sudden revelation: the melody Coltrane plays in the suite's concluding movement, "Psalm," follows syllable for syllable and word for word the devotional poem in the liner notes. In other words, the song Coltrane played was the poem he had written, as Porter soon proved by overdubbing a vocalist singing the poem's lyrics in unison with Coltrane's horn playing. As Coltrane launched his haunting, soul-stirring psalm heavenward, he was intoning in his mind's ear the words of his praise song. Here is part of the poem:

I will do all I can to be worthy of thee O lord
It has all to do with it.
Thank you God.
Peace.
There is none other.
God is. It is so beautiful.
Help us to resolve our fears and weaknesses.
Thank you God.
In you all things are possible.
We know. God made us so.
Keep your eye on God.
God is. He always was. He always will be.
No matter what . . . it is God.
He is most gracious and merciful.
It is most important that I know thee.
Words, sounds, speech, men, memory, thoughts, fears and emotions

— time — all related . . . all made from one . . . all made in one. Blessed be his name.[30]

The praise song is a vital component of every oral culture in which it is always a central expressive tool and focus. The song is a means of calling on one's gods, of invoking their presence, and of humbling oneself before the mystery of the unknown.

Music without words. Music with words. Music made of words. Words made of music. *A Love Supreme* is all of these and more. It symbolizes the tangled web of linguistic, political, and spiritual meanings that characterize the history of black music. It is at once an evocation of the wordless voice and its transcendence; an explicit celebration of Coltrane's oral heritage and the embodiment of its problematic condition; a spiritual affirmation that is neither Christian nor explicitly Afrocentric, yet draws on both in imagining a universal mysticism.

Just as the voice underlay the musical expressions of Africans, of African slaves in America, of blues singers and the drums of Congo Square, of Buddy Bolden's horn and Duke Ellington's orchestra, of bebop and free jazz, of the entire spectrum of music produced by black America, so too is the submerged voice at the heart of the culmination of that musical progression in the masterpiece that is *A Love Supreme*. The farther John Coltrane dug into himself, into his history and his music, the more profound was his reassertion of poetic orality. In his search for a context for his work, he reclaimed poetry's original organic context — the quest for spiritual identity — and in so doing made his final musical dedication to the realm of the human, the earthly, the material.

After the completion of *A Love Supreme*, Coltrane began a new phase in his life and music. After *A Love Supreme* came *Transitions*, *Om*, *Meditations*, *Ascension*, *Infinity*, *Expressions*, and *Interstellar Space*. Yet for John Coltrane, the key to this spiritual awakening was the praise song, his profession of personal devotion, the mystical union of the divine and human through song. Jazzman Bobby Timmons knew John Coltrane well:

> Once in a while I'd go back to Philadelphia to visit, and sometimes I'd talk with John's mother. I remember her telling me about *A Love Supreme* and how she was wishing he'd never written it. I

was surprised to hear her talking like that, but she told me John had a vision of God before he composed it. She also said John told her he was seeing these visions of God a lot of times when he was playing. She was worried to death, because, she said, "when someone is seeing God, that means he's going to die."[31]

John Coltrane died of cancer of the liver on July 17, 1967.

11 We Insist! Freedom Now Suite

MAX ROACH AND OSCAR BROWN JR.'S *Freedom Now Suite*, released in 1960 on Roach's Candid label, deserves to be considered, along with *A Love Supreme*, one of the greatest recordings in jazz, not only because of its exceptional musical importance, but because of its ambitious political and poetic summation of historical circumstances. If *A Love Supreme* is the record of one man's transformation from body to spirit, *Freedom Now Suite* is the record of a body that is all body, a record of transgressions against that body, of the anger, the hate, the sorrow, the dirt, and the hope that body has known for four hundred years. Like *A Love Supreme*, the individuals, events, passion, and context that created *Freedom Now Suite* form a whole with almost mythopoetical dimensions. The language, the music, the performers, and their lived history have a dramatic unity that lifts the suite beyond artistic expression to the realm of a revolutionary reordering of history.

Exactly what makes the *Freedom Now Suite* so compelling? To begin with, there is the appearance of Coleman Hawkins, who solos on the opening track, "Driva' Man." This recording was made in 1960; Hawkins, the man who virtually invented the jazz saxophone back in the 20s with the Fletcher Henderson Orchestra, is an old man here. He's seen it all. Felt it too. Highs and lows. And worse than that. But here he is, after all this time, up for the challenge, reinventing his own history. His horn drags its ragged ass across cotton fields. It growls like the dogs of the pattyrollers on his granddad's trail.

And the libretto, written by Oscar Brown Jr., sets the performers on fire. Its lyrics are agonizingly potent. They're exclamations, vocalized punctuations of the constant physical grind, the emotional anguish that constituted the life of a slave.

Driva' Man he made a life
but the woman ain't his wife
choppin' cotton don't be slow
better finish out your row
keep a movin' wit dat plow
driva' man'll show ya how
you get to work and root that stump
driva' man'll make you jump
better make your hammer ring
driva' man'll start to swing
ain't but two things on my mind
driva' man and quittin' time[32]

But those words, rich as they may be, are mere fuel for Abbey Lincoln's smouldering fire. If this page could sing with her voice, it would burn at your touch, leaving a sooty welt on your writhing palm.

The centrepiece of the *Freedom Now Suite* is a piece titled "Tryptych — Prayer/Protest/Peace." Again, "Tryptych" is an earthbound predecessor of Coltrane's "Love/Devotion/Surrender." It is an extended wordless duet by Max Roach and Abbey Lincoln, who were husband and wife at the time. They elect to forgo words — as did Coltrane — in this most profound assessment of their past — intuitively articulating the essential condition of jazz music as a wordless poetic language. Yet while Coltrane found his language, his poems, in the internalized praise song that is *A Love Supreme*, Roach and Lincoln eschew the inner path to transcendence, choosing instead to externalize their most private and volatile selves. The serenity Coltrane achieves at the end of his song is absent from "Tryptych." "Peace" means simply less suffering, less turmoil, less rage. Rather than sublime spirituality, for Roach "Peace" means "the feeling of relaxed exhaustion after you've done everything you can to assert yourself. You can rest now because you've worked to be free."[33]

"Tryptych" begins with "Prayer," a meditative vocal by Abbey Lincoln accompanied by Max Roach's sensual drumming. This is home. Safety. Africa. Suddenly, the "Protest" begins like a bolt of lightning. Roach pounds his snare furiously, and Lincoln screams and screams and screams, calling down galaxies of blood and pain: *Ahhhhhhhhhhhh! Ahhh! Ahhhhhhhh!* Then, just as unexpectedly, "Peace." Max, with muffled sticks on his toms, bayou trudging, click-click of insects. She sighs. She exhales like she's just fucked God. Time slides past the banks of a muddy river. It's all done.

Freedom Now Suite has several other movements, including "Freedom Day," "All Africa," and "Tears for Johannesburg." Although each is essential to the continuum of the suite and its overview of black American history and expression, none quite reaches the levels of cosmic intensity of "Tryptych." Yet there is no weak point on this album; it is a triumph in every sense. "All Africa," with Lincoln reciting the names of African tribes from whom American slaves were descended, accompanied by master drummer Babatunde Olatunji on percussion, who answers her tribal shouts with Yoruban chants, is a magnificently conceived and executed piece. And "Freedom Day," which captures the wonder, hope, fear, uncertainty, and infectious excitement of the day on which slaves discovered they were free, is also exceptional.

Inspired by the growing determination of black Americans to throw off the yoke of racist discrimination, by the bloodied Freedom Riders criss-crossing the south, by the courageous sit-ins and boycotts, and also by the lynchings, the church burnings, the snarling dogs, and water cannons of the bullying police, "We Insist!" demands *Freedom Now!* and is thus a singing arrow through the heart of oppression.

A Love Supreme and *Freedom Now Suite* signal the conclusion of a historical evolution that saw jazz evolve as the most potent public expression of black experience in America. Jazz gave voice both to the ancient African need for the affirmation of individual and communal identity in public song and the contemporary American need for black resistance and values to be articulated through musical metaphor. But jazz developed in a historical context that by the early 60s was undergoing radical change. Not only were social orthodoxies being challenged and social structures being reinvented, but the socio-musical trajectory that led from the work songs of slaves to the praise song that is *A Love Supreme* reached fruition isolated from popular black consciousness.

By the early 60s the musical anchor of black orality has shifted from jazz to R & B and Soul. And also at this time the white American voice comes dancing into the picture, leaping wildly into the surprised arms of black music and promising to re-oralize America. But before it does, let's turn back the clock and examine how and why black music had been a magnet for white words long before the birth of rock 'n' roll.

PART 2

Printopolis

12 The Forerunners of the New Bards

The Sick Man

Bands of Black men seem to be drifting in the air,
In the South, bands of thousands of Black men,
Playing mouth-organs in the night or, now, guitars.

Here in the North, late, late, there are voices of men,
Voices in chorus, singing without words, remote and deep,
Drifting choirs, long movements and turnings of sounds.

And in a bed, in one room, alone, a listener,
Waits for the unison of the music of the drifting bands,
And the dissolving chorals, waits for it and imagines

The words of winter in which these two will come together,
In the ceiling of the distant room, in which he lies,
The listener, listening to the shadows, seeing them.

Choosing out of himself, out of everything within him,
Speech for the quiet, good hail of himself, good hail, good hail,
The peaceful, blissful words, well-tuned, well-sung, well-spoken.

— WALLACE STEVENS[34]

DEPRIVED OF A FULLY FUNCTIONAL VOCABULARY, the oral imperatives that shaped African-American culture engendered a language whose external expression was musical yet whose internal logic was that of oral poetry. As the twentieth century progressed, the presence of this masked yet thriving poetry had a tremendous impact on white American poets, many of whom intuitively understood its essence. It was especially exciting to poets who felt the need to re-oralize poetry, to reclaim for poetry its lost music, its long-exiled voice, its absent body. Wallace Stevens's poem is just one of many examples of poems that point to the awareness of a parallel poetic universe in America, separate but equal in creative vitality to the poetry of the dominant literate culture, yet offering the key to an aesthetically and socially integrated poetic future. And this story is about the relationship between these two neighbouring poetries and their intertwined quests: black music searching for its words, and white poetry searching for its music, its body, its voice.

In Europe, poetry's oral heritage had been colonized, marginalized, entombed, or erased as the hegemony of textual authority grew in the centuries following Gutenberg's technological breakthrough. Increasingly, in the eighteenth and nineteenth centuries, regional dialects were abandoned or discriminated against, quasi-pagan rites and their popular poetries were prohibited, and established oral traditions (such as the druidic gathering of poets, the eisteddfod) fell into disfavour or were prohibited. Despite the valuable efforts of the first generations of proto-folkorists in the mid- and late nineteenth century — chasing down legendary epics, ancient folktales, and village poems — it would take a revolution before the notion of re-embodying poetry would be publicly proclaimed and enacted. And one was in the offing as the shadow of the great war loomed. In that revolution, in the ecstatic experimentation and apocalyptic aesthetics of Dadaists and Futurists, with their sound poems, their polyvocal poems in multiple languages, their aleatory poems, their guerrilla poems, their muscular poems, their shit-smeared poems — the embers of Europe's living oral folk poetries glow only dimly. Europe was being made new as it came apart at the seams, and in the tumult the shouting poets were focused wholly on the future, on invention, new words, new forms, new meanings. Every traditional alternative was perceived as either corrupt or dead by Mayakovsky, by Marinetti, by Schwitters. And despite the flickers of oral potential — despite Joyce's singsong peat-bog arcana and Gertrude Stein's repetitious ragas, which spoke volumes before there were ears to hear — the momentum had shifted to the New World. America was calling and soon Europe would listen. Soon the entire world would listen. And dance.

In America everything was up for grabs. Music without words. Words without music. In America. Where any dream was possible. Where, even as Protestant provincialists clung fast to hidebound tradition, the future was beckoning like an untilled field. Where during its greatest upheaval, the civil war, America's revolutionary fertility yielded an extraordinary poetry, born of the earth yet reaching toward a visionary future, a maverick oeuvre based on a dream of spiritual, sexual, and aesthetic transformation cast against the backdrop of an evolving self-defining national utopia. America had called to life a poet to whom freedom meant freedom to create the future, not to escape from the past. America had birthed Walt Whitman.

As the apostle of personal and aesthetic revolution Whitman abandoned the typographic poem and reasserted the primacy of the spoken poem, the sung word, the songs of the body electric. He could hardly have done otherwise, even though by profession he was a printer. Quatrains, sestinos, and sonnets, though fashionable, could no more have contained Whitman's heaving spirit than they could have contained his loafing, electric soul. Rather than parse, Whitman chose to dance:

> I celebrate myself, and sing myself,
> And what I assume you shall assume,
> For every atom belonging to me as good belongs to you.[35]

Whitman was the first and greatest prophet of the liberated body, of the kinetic sensuality of everyday speech, of transcendent public song in America, but he was not the last. Far from it. Whitman believed he was living in the promised land, that he was the nation made flesh, that his prophecies could and would be realized. Those who followed him, however, understood themselves as intermediaries between the real and the sublime. And yet their electric words flowed. New songs were always sung.

In contrast to disenfranchised black musicians, white American poets in the century following the civil war possessed their word-language in its entirety. They had at their fingertips more words than they might ever conceivably use, yet the typographic imperative that literally shaped their poems excluded the natural music of the speaking voice. Print had long since severed the body from poetry, and along with it all the contextualizing infrastructure of oral communication: time, space, community, ritual, sensuality, chance, dance, dialogue, aching feet, the weather. And yet, this literate chasm between poet and poem, between poet and audience, between intellectual appreciation and bodily sensation, between creation and distribution, was resisted and subverted by a class of poets who felt the incipient desire to reawaken the singing voice in poetry. When these keen-eared and broad-minded American poets encountered the potent poetic stew that was jazz, their interest was immediately sparked.

One such maverick was Vachel Lindsay, who, at the turn of the twentieth century, sang and recited his poems as he tramped across America "trading rhymes for bread." He was no great poet, yet he was the best-known American poet of his day. "I write for an audience of three million," he boasts in the preface to his collected poems, published in 1925. And, as he also enjoyed proclaiming, he had recited his poems to a million or more townspeople, labourers, students, and sundry other citizens during his extensive travels across North America. Yet Lindsay hesitated. Despite his one million auditors, he insisted, "All my verses marked to be read aloud should be whispered, however contradictory that might seem. All poetry is first and last for the inner ear, and its final pleasures are for the soul, whispering in solitude." His poems, he says doggedly, "contain no jazz, spasm or irregularity,"[36]despite a widespread critical perception that this was in fact the case. Although he wrote many poems based on "Negro" life, and Negro religious activity in particular, Lindsay's perception of that life was pathetically narrow-minded, and profoundly racist. One of his most famous poems is *The Congo (A Study of the Negro Race)*, whose three sections are subtitled "Their Basic Savagery," "Their Irrepressible High Spirits," and "The Hope of Their Religion."

Lindsay disclaimed all traces of jazz influence in his work, and yet Lindsay's head and heart — or more accurately his head and ear — were at war:

> My father had a musical voice, and he used to read us Uncle Remus, and he could sing every scrap of song therein and revise every story by what some old slave had told him. He used to sing the littler children to sleep with negro melodies which he loved, and which negroes used to sing to him, when they rocked him to sleep in his infancy. We nearly always had a Black hired man and a Black hired girl. My father took us to Jubilee singer concerts from Fisk or Hampton, and came home rendering the songs authentically and from boyhood memory. Moreover our negro servants did not hesitate to sing.[37]

Several points are worth noting in this description. First, Lindsay's father must not be construed as a liberal or abolitionist. Lindsay goes on to say: "The Mason-Dixon line ran straight through our house in Springfield, Illinois, and straight through my heart. No man may escape his bouncing infancy."[38] Lindsay's father had been a slave owner and was dead set against Lincoln's emancipation movement.

Second, Lindsay's reminiscence was not intended to shed light on the origins of his songmaking, but rather to explain how he happened to have such a "familiarity" with "negroes." Lindsay drew no connection whatsoever between the "negro" songs and stories that informed his childhood and his proclivity for writing and reciting poems that others consistently asserted were influenced by jazz. Reading Lindsay's lengthy, rambling introduction to his collected poems, one immediately senses a mind that in its unchecked fulsomeness easily misses its target as often as hits it. And so it is with his assessment of his work's lack of jazz spasm. He got it wrong, dead wrong, because he was blinded by his deeply ingrained sense of racial superiority.

For poets, print has been a mixed blessing. On the one hand, print has allowed poets to communicate with each other, and with audiences across continents and centuries. But in that process of communication, something has been lost: the body, the voice, the poet as actor, as an active force in the life of a community. Some poets are content to modify their poems and poetic aims to fit the typographic mindset, and others have poetic proclivities that drive them inexorably toward embracing the role of poet as actor. Many of the best American poets of the twentieth century have belonged to the latter group, as did most certainly Carl Sandburg, who celebrated black American music with passion and insight in such poems as "Jazz Fantasia:"

Drum on your drums, batter on your banjos,
Sob on the long cool winding saxophones,
Go to it O jazzmen.

Sling your knuckles on the bottoms of the happy
tin pans, let your trombones ooze, and go husha-
husha-hush with the slippery sandpaper...[39]

Sandburg, songmaker to the world, walking the ragged smoky alleys of Chicago, chasing the sounds of rivermen rocking through gin joints, the old jazz, the old Chicago jazz, with its xylophones, its barnyard calls, its whoops and stomps, the mouth-music of the New World, and Sandburg, the wandering minstrel, all eyes and ears on top of a mountain on top of a skyscraper on top of a guitar, singing to America.

In 1927, Sandburg published his now-revered folk song anthology, *The American Songbag* — 280 songs collected by a man who spent decades singing and learning songs across the country. It is not the poetry of institutions, libraries, or academies, but of working people, lovers, babes, and criminals. Sandburg loved these songs for their physicality, their intimacy, their narrative power, and he was drawn to jazz for the same reasons.

Like Lindsay, Sandburg spent many years as a wandering poet. His later fame was preceded first by obscurity and a little later by notoriety as his early work began to be read in magazines like Harriet Monroe's *Poetry*, in which he appeared as early as 1914. During those early years, as Sandburg gained local recognition as a troubadour of skill and integrity, he wrote his greatest poems — poems like "Chicago" and "The Sins of Kalamazoo," which bellow and howl with all the passion of Whitman before him and Ginsberg after. Sandburg's poems call out for the voice, for embodiment. His cadences are those of speech and his intonation that of everyday life. Sandburg was probably one of the first white men to sing the blues in public without blackface on, although there were many, like Vachel Lindsay's father, who sang them to their children in private. In fact, Sandburg's brief descriptions of how he came to collect the blues songs in *The American Songbag* are nearly all identical:

In Duluth, Minnesota, I heard Margaret Moore Nye, of a Richmond, Virginia family, deliver this spiritual as she heard it in the kitchen of her girlhood home.[40]

A North Carolina woman at Purdue University heard this for years as a girl from a negro woman cook in her home. "Often when I was in the kitchen she would say to me, 'Come on Miss Mary, get on de tune wagon, you ain't on de tune wagon.'"[41]

Florence Heizer of Osage, Kansas, heard this often from a negro woman, who, over the ironing board, could reply to any mourning dove that sat in the cottonwoods.[42]

Tubman K. Hendrick heard this often from a hotel kitchen in Memphis, over and over, day after day.[43]

This arrangement is based on the song as heard at the Wisconsin Player's House in Milwaukee, where it arrived through an Oklahoma poet named Ellis, who heard it from negroes in the cotton fields of Texas.[44]

Sandburg describes one particular song, " Those Gambler Blues," as what polite society calls a gutter song. "In a foreign language, in any lingo but that of the U.S.A., it would seem less vulgar, more bizarre. Its opening realism works on towards irony and fantasy, dropping in its final lines again to blunt realism."[45] Did Carl Sandburg, poet laureate of white America, understand the blues? Damn right. He loved them. And learned from them. Of course he did. He was an American poet. In this evocative poem, Sandburg's longing for a poetry of the body and spirit is implicitly linked to the trauma of displacement underlying black experience:

Singing Nigger

Your bony head, O Jazbo, O dock walloper,
Those grappling hooks, those wheelbarrow handlers,
The dome and the wings of you, nigger,
the red roof and the door of you,

I know where your songs come from.
I know why God listens to your, " Walk All Over God's Heaven."
I heard you shooting craps, "My baby's going to have a new dress."
I heard you in the cinders, "I'm going to live anyhow until I die."
I saw five of you with a can of beer on a summer night and
I listened to the five of you harmonizing six ways
to sing, " Way Down Yonder in the Cornfield."
I went away asking where I come from.[46]

Sandburg was a revolutionary, not because for many years he was a socialist organizer (although poets of the voice tend to be more politically radical and engaged than poets of the page), but because he instinctively trumpeted the poetry of the body and the voice over the poetry of the page. Inspired in part by black oral culture, he was an apostle of the revolution of the living word, a revolution that continued to intensify even after his own poetry sank into trivial, patriotic torpor.

Our story — this thread of our story — does not end here, but it pauses, to be taken up again only after two world wars have shaken the planet. The American poet as extrovert, as rambler and ranter, as actor, will spend the years between the wars in hibernation or exile. But what of Louis Zukofsky and Delmore Schwartz, of Edna Millay, Hart Crane, and e.e. cummings? Yes, indeed, what of American poets during the Jazz Age and the Great Depression?

There seems to be a kernel of truth somewhere in suggesting that the Whitmans and Sandburgs of the world appeal to the listener-as-body, whereas the cummingses and Zukofskys appeal to the listener-as-mind. Might it be that some poets aim to engage the outer, public, physical ear, and through it the corporeal being of the listener, while others appeal to the inner, private ear of the imagination? One poet challenges, the other seduces? Even e.e. cummings, for all his body and flower imagery, remains a private poet whose words are meant to ring within the listener, not without. As do Delmore Schwartz's, or Hart Crane's vulnerable incantations. Perhaps the question is one of self-confidence. This poet demands an audience, while that poet tolerates or even dreads one. This poet defies, that poet despairs. One exclaims to transform the outer world, the other whispers to alter the inner domain. Perhaps this story, the story of those poets with the confidence and desire to speak their verse publicly, to challenge the external world with their own body, with their own embodied poetic voice — pauses between the wars out of necessity to give birth to a new generation. For Sandburg was not yet alienated as a young poet; he still believed in America's potential, in Whitman's America, in the possibility of Progress as a moral force. Those poets who followed, who lived through the great wars as adults, as participants, like cummings, Schwartz, and Crane, retreated to the private realm, unable to heal the wounds to their faith in the future of the body.

In a 1936 article titled "Public Speech and Private Speech in Poetry," Archibald MacLeish, one of the most articulate and engaged poets of his era, wrote:

> The poets of our time to whom the revolution in poetry was unreal, or who were unable for one reason or another to profit by it, have found themselves face to face with a brutal choice — to resign either from their age or from their art. Many of them, unable to comprehend within a rhetorical (pre-modern) art a generation of violence and tragedy and menace, have been driven either out of their art into silence, or out of their age into dreams.[47]

By the time Patchen, Ginsberg, and the next generation of poets had matured, they had internalized that pain and sought to reaffirm the body, the voice, the future of physical reality in a negation of established conventions, a negation of the American ideal. Like Schwartz and Crane, they were alienated, but unlike them, they were alienated from birth, and so had the strength to challenge, to defy, and to reclaim the voice of the poet. They looked out, away from the wounds, and they sang of a dream defiled. There was nothing left to be afraid of. The worst had already happened. The future was now.

MacLeish praised the work of the proletarian poets of the 30s, many of whom, like Joy Davidman or Stanley Burnshaw or Thomas McGrath, were capable of writing compact and beautiful poems that sought to capture the vitality of the spoken idioms of the day. Perhaps as a result of the limitations of the times, rather than to any defect of their person or poetry, they were unable to effect the revolution *in sound* demanded by the imminent resurgence of oral poetry. MacLeish writes:

> Tentative though it may now be, it is, nevertheless, probable that this transition toward a poetry capable of accepting a political and revolutionary era upon its own terms is a transition capable, if effected, of reaching the greatest and most noble ends — the true ends of poetry — the ends of all the greatest poetry of the past. It is a transition capable of restoring a poetry of public speech.[48]

It was a poetry of public speech that American poets, both black and white, were desperately striving for.

13 Song of a Poet

PARIS. MARCH 12, 1929. Jean Cocteau reads two poems from *Opera* ("La Toison d'or" and "Les Voleurs d'enfants") accompanied by Dan Parrish and his orchestra. Little, if anything, can prepare the listener for an initial audition of Jean Cocteau's recitation of "La Toison d'or." Cocteau's performance, accompanied by a loose and swinging eight-piece jazz ensemble, was unprecedented. And it remains in certain respects the jazz and poetry collaboration against which all others must be judged.

But before assessing the work itself, consider for a moment the extraordinary strangeness of the event having occurred at all. Cocteau was in Pathe's Paris recording studio on a March afternoon in 1929 to record six selections from his well-received collection of poems, *Opera*. This fact in itself is highly unusual, for few poets of Cocteau's era thought it important to record their work. Cocteau, however, did. So we find the poet in the studio, having completed the first four of his a cappella recitations. Hanging around the control booth, or lounging in the corridor outside an adjacent recording studio perhaps, are the members of the Dan Parrish Orchestra, a jazz band made up of both visiting and expatriate black American musicians. Displaying his characteristic moxie and his intuitive brilliance, Cocteau suggests that the musicians accompany him for the final two poems. Cocteau's record producers are outraged. *Quel scandale!* But they finally agree to humour the notorious eccentric, with the proviso that the recordings would never see the light of day. (And they wouldn't for over fifty years.)

So Cocteau brought in the band. Did they rehearse? I don't believe that they spent more than five minutes figuring out what to do. For if Cocteau hadn't instinctively understood his role, then no amount of rehearsal could have taught him. The machines were turned on, and the band launched into a number called "Holidays." Cocteau then miraculously proceeded to become a member of the band, a featured soloist on — French poetry. And, man, could he blow! His solo is impeccable. It begins with a tricky two-bar break he nails with these words: "Boucleé, boucleé, l'antiquité."

Cocteau swings beautifully. Moreover, Cocteau's poem mirrors the formal logic of the song. Here his voice riffs over a transitional turnaround; there he is silent while the band briefly changes moods; here he jumps back in again, with a concluding three lines leading elegantly to the tune's finale. His voice is clear and concise as he plays with pitch and volume. The colour is provided by the extensive inner rhymes and alliteration of the poem. He is a jazzman.

How did Cocteau manage it? Jazz had been heard in Paris for a decade, but the idea that a Frenchman with little exposure to black music of any kind — remember, this was 1929, and black music still sounded like it came from Mars to most Europeans — could simply waltz in and instantly become a jazz poet is astounding. Even acknowledging that Cocteau was an artistic polymath, the distance he travelled in those few brief minutes was so great that decades would pass before anyone else achieved the same degree of integration between jazz and poetry-as-poetry. How does it fit into our story? It doesn't. It is an aberration, utterly without influence. And yet it is a sign, a curious, scandalous sign of things to come.

14 William Carlos Williams and the New World Idiom

William Carlos Williams was in many ways the quintessential American poet. His most famous poetic dictum was "no poems but in things." But this poetic materialism was not uniquely American. Williams is an American poet, above all because of the particular structure, tone, and rhythm of his poems. It's how his poems feel. How *do* his poems feel?

An Exercise

Sick as I am
confused in the head
I mean I have

endured this April
so far
visiting friends

returning home
late at night
I saw

a huge Negro
a dirty collar
about his

enormous neck
appeared to be
choking

him
I did not know
whether or not

he saw me though
he was sitting
directly

before me how
shall we
escape this modern

age
and learn
to breathe again[49]

Williams was a first-generation American poet struggling to find his voice, a voice he perceived as almost entirely removed from the European tradition. And yet neither the process nor the poetic principles he elaborated were as unique as they appeared to literary critics, for many of the same influences were even then shaping the evolution of jazz. In an essential and yet for the most part unacknowledged way, the poetry of William Carlos Williams is inextricably linked to jazz.

The feel of Williams's poems, that fresh yet elusive fluidity, has always been associated with his idiosyncratic approach to rhythm. Williams called his rhythmic method the *variable foot*, an enigmatic phrase that has confounded students for decades. Stephen Cushman opens his book *William Carlos Williams and the Meaning of Measure* with a statement of the problem:

Beginning with his essay "Speech Rhythms" (1913), in which he declares "time, not the syllables, must be counted," Williams crusaded on behalf of his theory of measure for nearly fifty years. During that time, a period that extended from the infancy of modernism to the emergence of the contemporary poetic generation, his theory of measure grew beyond prosody into mythology ... Williams found himself and his theory haunted by contradictions. The larger the measure grew the harder it became to define. Was it primarily auditory or was it also visual? Could it be counted, or simply felt? Did it approximate quantitative meter or musical time, or did it define some other kind of meter or time? Faced with such questions and inconsistencies, many of Williams' readers and critics have had to lead double-lives, admiring his poems while apologizing for his theory. Those well-meaning readers who have set out not to apologize, but rather to explain, have found themselves hypnotized by Williams' logic and terminology, until soon they are solemnly repeating his slogans or formulations.[50]

Were Stephen Cushman a jazz drummer, he'd have little trouble deciphering the variable foot. By keeping time with drummer's feet, he'd understand that William Carlos Williams's poetry swings. Not in the manner of the clunky jazz poems that clutter quasi-hip literary anthologies, but rather as a field holler swings with an inexorable impulsion. Pound's definition of rhythm as a form cut into time is less appropriate a definition of swing, in poetry or in jazz, than that of a form buoyed up by time. A form shaped and borne along by the human breath. Why should the poetry of a New Jersey village doctor, a man who never paid any attention to jazz in his life, swing? Because he was a mama's boy.

Williams's mother was, by her son's admission, the most significant influence on his life. He even wrote her biography, *Yes, Mrs. Williams: A Personal History of My Mother.* Born in Puerto Rico of Spanish and French parentage, with Spanish as her native tongue, Elena Williams did not begin to learn English until she moved to America in 1882, the year she gave birth to William Carlos. Although Williams's father was British, he spoke Spanish, according to his son, better than most

Spaniards. So the poet heard Spanish around the house in his early childhood.

Williams's mother was spiritually inclined. She experienced ecstatic trances, occasionally acted as a medium, and sometimes spoke in tongues. Williams idolized her. She had been impressed at an early age by the Spiritualist trend then making rounds of the Puerto Rican upper classes, to which she belonged. When she was eight, however, her father died and left her alone with her brother and mother. The family struggled financially and as a result was frequently in contact thereafter with "lower" elements in society. Mrs. Williams's interest in the supernatural was further encouraged in her new environment, where non-Christian beliefs flourished unchecked by Catholicism.

Williams treasured the multiracial and multicultural aspect of his heritage:

> In the west indies, in Martinique, Saint Thomas, Puerto Rico, Santo Domingo, in those days, the races of the world mingled and intermarried — imparting their traits one to another and forgetting the orthodoxy of their ancient and medieval views. It was a good thing. It is in the best spirit of the New World.[51]

We do not know to what extent Elena Williams participated in Afro-Caribbean religious ceremonies. It is possible that she found herself drawn to local religious events during which, in the garbled languages of their African ancestors, freed slaves invoked their ancient *loas* in song and dance. Were those Yoruban incantations to Ogun ringing down the deserted streets of Patterson, New Jersey, years later when Mrs. Williams had one of her "episodes"?

Even after she had emigrated, when she was speaking in her adopted local tongue, English, we may justifiably wonder what manner of language came out of Mrs. Williams's mouth. In a remarkable section of Kerry Driscoll's book, *William Carlos Williams and the Maternal Muse*, the author links Williams's poetic sensibility to his mother's speech habits:

> Moreover, it was in his mother's hybrid dialect — that curious melange of colloquial expressions, foreign words and non-standard syntax — that the poet found his key to the possession of America ... His description of Elena's speech sounds remarkably

similar to his description of the American idiom: [It is] not English, but a new start from a new base.[52]

Driscoll goes on to analyze one of Williams's handwritten notebooks in which he transcribes his mother's words into 3-line stanzas resembling his own poetry. Following one of these stanzas, the poet queries: " Where I got my line?"

Elena Williams's linguistic eccentricities were a product of her intercultural identity and experience. Here we can see a direct link between Williams's poetry and jazz, as it was the fusion of African and European cultures and voices in America that gave birth to both. And if Williams acknowledges that his mother's hybrid dialect may be the source of his line, of his variable foot, and if jazz too is a hybrid dialect born of the collision of cultures in the New World, then a sibling-like relationship between Williams's poetry and jazz ought to be apparent when they are placed side by side. And so it is.

You can hear it on an unusual recording of Williams's poem " Tract." This recording, made in 1958 and released on the World Pacific album *Jazz Canto Vol. 1*, features Hoagy Carmichael reading the poem accompanied by jazz bassist Ralph Pena's quintet. This performance, just over five minutes in duration, is one of the most compelling recorded examples of poetic recitation accompanied by jazz. It may also be the most compelling articulation of Williams's poetry, in *any* form, including writing.

Hoagy Carmichael was not so much a jazz musician as a musician who played jazz and played it well. He worked in the 1920s with Louis Armstrong and later with celebrated boppers like Art Pepper and Sweets Edison. Carmichael's Indiana birthplace, his tremendous native musicality, and his steadfast aesthetic populism were all reflected in his rich baritone drawl, a singing voice at once casual yet satisfying, stripped of pretension, polished yet naturalistic, and ideal for Williams's poetry. Although he retained the musical respect of many black jazz musicians for his well-crafted songs, that Carmichael also occasionally stooped to writing "coon songs" shows that in this sense he was deeply representative of the mainstream white attitude toward black culture.

Hoagy Carmichael was a skilled and occasionally inspired songwriter. He often wrote his own lyrics as well as music, and in such perennial favourites as "Skylark," "Lazy River," and "Georgia on My

Mind," Carmichael displayed a high degree of understanding of the relations between words and music. Because he so embodied the popular American sense of rhythm, melody, and tone of voice, he was ideally suited to express the crystalline robustness of William Carlos Williams's poetry.

The recording in question begins with a simple melody played on the guitar, accompanied by a bowed double bass. It is a slow, loping melody — simple and engaging. Soon the melody ends and is replaced by a distant and ominous snare-drum march. Carmichael begins speaking:

Tract

I will tell you my townspeople
how to perform a funeral
for you have it over a troop
of artists —
unless you should scour the world —
you have the groundsense necessary...[53]

Carmichael's voice is every bit as challenging and admonishing as the text. Over the course of the poem, his voice shifts, becoming wry or angry, disdainful or encouraging as necessitated. But throughout his voice retains an extraordinary naturalness, which is the source of its power. The poem sounds entirely spontaneous and thus achieves that intimacy and immediacy for which Williams always strove. After several lines, on cue, the musicians return and the guitarist begins to elaborate a melancholy, bluesy solo around his original lyrical melody. Carmichael takes absolutely no notice, or seems not to. He continues his dramatic monologue with the same rhythmic intensity with which he began, apparently oblivious to the group. Yet it is precisely his rhythmic confidence, the urgent musical demands of his speaking voice, that propels the ensemble forward. The musicians respond with their own rhythmic confidence; joining in support of the voice, buoying it as it sets out to swallow, circle, splice, sway, and strangle the beat; as it marks the measure with the caesuras of intonation and breath; as "it envelopes each phrase which is destined to speak to the soul" — a line borrowed from Francis Bebey, for whom it describes the essence of the African sense of rhythm.

Carmichael swings Williams's poem with a rhythmic sophistication to be found only in the most polyrhythmic of musical idioms. Or in everyday speech. He never emphasizes the beat, or even acknowledges it. Like a master drummer, he straddles the beat, twists it, and twines it, leaving it pulsing in the wake of his voice. No jazz musician could fail to hear in this activity, or in the intense lyricism and spontaneous invention of his spoken melody, a direct kinship with the expressive aims of his own art. Musician and poem share a similitude of syntax, of tone, and of rhythm. They both swing. And they both swing for the same reasons.

15 Beats and Riffs

The strange note makes the trumpeter of the band lift an eyebrow
Dizzy is surprised for the first time that day
he puts the trumpet to his lips and blows a wet blur
Hee-hee-ha laughs Charlie Parker bending down to slap his ankle
He puts his alto to his mouth and says "didn't I tell you?" with jazz
of notes
talking eloquent like great poets of foreign languages singing in
foreign countries with lyres by seas
and no one understands because the language isn't alive in the
land yet
bop is the language from America's inevitable Africa[54]

— JACK KEROUAC

So what have we got here? A guy, a regular joe, a writer, a lover, a drifter, a football player, a Catholic French Canadian from New England, a guy who dug jazz, a blower, a lush, a bitter old-before-his-time bigot, a corpse.

But in his day Jack Kerouac was the real thing, a great American poet. An ofay poet who truly understood jazz. But he fooled a lot of people over the years. He tricked up the jazz fans and critics by writing poems about jazz musicians in which he got all the facts wrong. Lionel

Hampton wasn't a sax player. Charlie Parker a Buddha? Not by the account of anyone who knew him. Kerouac dug bop, which is as it should be. But he didn't know jazz as music, he knew it as poetry, which is why he misled everyone who knew jazz as only music. They thought he was full of crap, but he had a handle on a level of jazz expression the critics had missed. He listened only to the musicians' voices, oblivious to scales and tempos and notes. And his own voice shows how well he listened; how much music he had in him; how all he listened for, even in writing, was music. The music of speech, shouts, come-ons, and drunken proclamations. Of silences. Of sex. Of steel-wheeled railroads and stupefying ramblings in the cosmic American night.

What Ti-Jean got right about jazz, what he learned from it and later articulated to Ginsberg and his cohorts, was the ability to listen — *ear power*. In listening to jazz musicians, Kerouac learned better how to listen. And in better learning to listen, he better learned how to speak. As jazz musicians would say, *he had big ears*.

Kerouac was a writer. This is what he said about writing: "A true writer should be an observer and not go around *being* observed, like Mailer and Ginsberg. Observing — that's the duty and oath of a writer."[55] But he wasn't only a writer. On his three albums, and always in his mind's ear, Kerouac was also a speaker — an oral poet. So if observing is the duty and oath of a writer, then what is the duty and oath of an oral poet?

Listening.

Kerouac knew that Bird and Dizzy and Monk were poets. He knew they were foreign dignitaries whose "language wasn't alive in the land yet." But he didn't care to study the translations. He just listened, learned, then carved a place for his unadorned voice and sang. What more can one say of a poet? And what less?

Allen Ginsberg tagged Kerouac's idiom "spontaneous bop prosody." Ginsberg — who would later record with many jazz and rock 'n' roll musicians — learned about black music from Kerouac. As he later said, "'Lester Leaps In.' *Howl* is all 'Lester Leaps In.' And I got that from Kerouac. Or paid attention to it on account of Kerouac — surely, he made me listen to it."[56]

Bird and Dizzy were dignitaries discoursing in a foreign tongue, Kerouac was a brilliant itinerant who gave up and went home, but Ginsberg, disciple of the body-voice, devourer of the omnivorous

American poetic stew, was a loud and lascivious American boy in full possession of his national language — with poetic mayhem on his mind.

It was Ginsberg's triumph that he heard in his mind's ear the poems signalling a shift in the balance of power between the voice and the page. After Ginsberg and his numerous cohorts, there was no turning back. The teenagers, the children, the babies, would, in ever greater numbers, turn away from the page and to the song, the stage, the body. Not that one man was responsible for this shift, nor that in Molefi Kete Asante's words, the "psychic stain of Africa" was its sole cause. And yet, Ginsberg embodies the transition from an inchoate poetic orality that enjoyed an uneasy kinship with black music, to an overt celebration, a loud shouting, a bardic tribute to the body, and to the jazz and blues poets whose voices had been singing in the wilderness for many years. Ginsberg was — in retrospect — the first white rock star.

Not that anybody knew this at the time. Not even when Ginsberg and his beat and post-beat peers began performing with bands in the late 50s, kick-starting a fad that would briefly sweep hip America. In fact, the popularity of jazz-and-poetry collaborations was so great that nightclubs and college campuses across America in 1957 were regularly featuring their versions of "the new thing." The fusion of jazz and poetry was, however, roundly attacked by critics of both disciplines. It was seen by jazz critics as an unnecessary and fruitless shotgun wedding of two incompatible artistic traditions and by the more conservative literary critics as the bastard child of an artistic discipline and a primitive caterwauling.

To be fair to those who hated the new form, however, there was undoubtedly much to dislike. While this book sets out to show how closely jazz and poetry are related on profound levels, their integration on the superficial level has always presented sophisticated practical challenges. Poets ignorant of those challenges, who blindly declaimed their "jazz verses" with little preparation or musical rehearsal, have often produced collaborations that weaken rather than strengthen the respective idioms. Yet to be fair to the critics of the critics, highbrow attacks on such collaborations were usually motivated by bigotry, ignorance, and fear as much as by any artistic criteria.

Because for those willing to listen closely and to seek out the best work, some terrific stuff was being done. Some of it appears on *Poetry Readings at the Cellar*. One side of the album features Lawrence

Ferlinghetti and the other Kenneth Rexroth. Both poets took their performative roles seriously and as a result produced memorable work. On the liner notes to the album, Ferlinghetti wrote:

> When you do it this way, the poetry reads better as a result. Once it goes through the test, this oral test, then if it makes it that way, you don't have to worry about it on the page. It will read well silently too. The big thing is the oral message. My whole kick has been oral poetry. The poets today are talking to themselves, they have no other audience ... Poetry used to have an audience. Lindsay went around the country reciting poems for bread — that was his phrase. And Sandburg, when he was younger, went around with a guitar and had an audience. We're trying to capture an audience. Gutenberg had a good idea but it ran away from him and ruined it for the poets.[57]

Ferlinghetti's "Autobiography," which appears on the LP, is a supremely successful music and poetry collaboration. "Autobiography" was written to be performed with a band. The format is simple: Ferlinghetti and the jazz quintet "trade fours." That is to say they exchange improvised four-bar solos in the same way jazz players do. Of course, Ferlinghetti's solos are neither improvised nor four bars long. Some stanzas are longer and some are shorter. Yet though the length of the solos is inconsistent, the musicians who must listen and come in on cue have little difficulty doing so, for the rhythm of the poet's voice is organically linked to their jazz rhythms.

Ferlinghetti's tone is eminently casual, as if he's relating an anecdote late at night in a bar to a few friends. Which is exactly what he is doing. (How exciting, that poetry should *sound* at home in its home of the moment! Surely that ought to be one of the fundamental goals of poets, to speak directly to the community in the community's own voice.) Through heightened idiomatic speech, idiosyncratic images, and insightful observations, Ferlinghetti creates an irrepressibly engaging and accessible poetic saga.

The popular fusion of jazz and poetry on stage and on record in the beat era resurrected the notion that poetry should be popular. As Rexroth puts it: "Homer, or the guy who recited Beowulf, was show business. We simply want to make poetry a part of show business."[58]

16 Rock 'n' Roll

ROCK 'N' ROLL IS A FREAK OF HISTORY, an omni-present populist poetic idiom, an anarchic, amorphous, open-ended circus of personas, rhythms, and hormones. It is an oral culture in full effect; profoundly democratic, pluralistic, and fluid. Rock 'n' roll is the American Dream made flesh. It is the return of Walt Whitman, prancing about in spandex stars-and-stripes hot pants with a Stratocaster slung about his neck. It is a national pulse.

I mean this literally. Rock 'n' roll is the revolution of the American body. It is the reconciliation of the American body and the American imagination in song. It is the realization and fulfillment of the search for wholeness in poetry. But only for some. Only for white folks. Ironically, for black folks, who invented rock 'n' roll in the first place, who inadvertently supplied young white Americans with the music that galvanized their struggle for liberation from a deadening socio-cultural straitjacket, the reunion of music with the word would require still more patience.

Rock 'n' roll, to begin at the beginning, is black music. It emerged as a distinct musical form — or family of forms — following the great mid-century schism that saw jazz diverge into two related yet distinct camps: art music and pop music. The art music was "modern" jazz, that is to say, post-swing jazz. Initially, this meant bebop, a stylistic threshold so stark and so influential that for many young jazz musicians today it constitutes a veritable big bang, before which little else is thought to have existed. The second path, that of pop music, consisted of jump blues, R&B, and eventually rock'n'roll. Although there would be regular intercourse between the two realms — both John Coltrane and Ornette Coleman, for example, toured with R & B bands as young men — a permanent rift in black music had taken place by mid-century.

Before the schism, jazz was both art music and pop music. It was party music, dance music, and screwing music at the same time as it was intellectually challenging, aesthetically sophisticated, and subtly individualistic artistic expression. Jazz musicians pushed themselves to the limit of their creative and technical imaginations in the service of music that was typically performed in dancehalls and nightclubs. For their efforts, they were applauded and supported by a relatively knowledgeable endorphin-saturated public. Jazz was a good time. It was showbiz. Duke Ellington, Cab Calloway, Chick Webb, Count Basie, Fletcher Henderson — all the big band leaders understood this, as did individual musician-entertainers like Hot Lips Page, Louis Armstrong, Jack Teagarden, Stuff Smith, Sonny Greer, and countless others. These jazz players were comfortable as both artist and entertainer, and they felt no creative contradiction or artistic compromise in their dual roles. They understood that some people would listen more than others, that everybody was there for a good time, that music —the most important thing to a musician — was only one part of the larger whole that was the public social event. They had an intuitive understanding, derived from the still powerful adherence of the black community to oral values, of their place in the grand scheme of things, and they embraced that respected position without bitterness.

The years just before the schism — the late 30s and early 40s — were the heyday of the big bands, whose easy swinging conversations between horn, brass, and rhythm sections reinforced and reflected the communalism inherent in black music. And yet, as mutually satisfying as was this relationship between artist and community, a handful of younger players were dissatisfied with it. These musicians wanted more out of the music — much of which had grown diluted and dull as it was embraced by and refashioned for the mainstream (read: white) American market — and they didn't care whether people listened or not. They wanted, to begin with, longer solos; more substantial opportunities to express themselves than were possible as a member of an eighteen-piece band. So they formed small groups, and they took long, long solos. And they wanted to play faster music, music that reflected the accelerated pace of the world around them, music that was more challenging technically; they didn't care if people danced, they didn't want people to dance, they just wanted to push the limits of their own creative abilities. These younger players had worked their instruments in ways that none of the older cats had ever imagined. They could play *fast.* So they did. Tempos that had never before been attempted in jazz became their bread and butter. Four beats a second. Five beats a second. All built on polyrhythmic foundations supplied by unpredictable and lightning-quick drummers. Their furious rhythm-n-ing discouraged most old-timers but inspired youngsters to take their playing to a new level.

In addition to playing long, fast solos, they introduced a third innovation that would prove definitive: complex chord changes. In the swing era, chord changes were for the most part limited to simple progressions of simple chords. In bebop — for that is what these young lions found their music being called — a given chorus might see dozens of chords interwoven, including newfangled chords with odd notes such as flat ninths and flat fifths and suspended fourths. Finally, then, with its confusing blur of unfamiliar chord changes, its frenetic nearly undanceable tempi, and its extended solos, bebop was complete. Created by dissatisfied misfits as an individualistic alternative to the predominant communalist, entertainment-oriented, socio-musical paradigm, the results were predictable. It was self-consciously, undeniably, irresponsibly *art* — and most people, both black and white, hated it.

Thus the schism.

Bebop was an extraordinary artistic achievement. But that is all it was. This is not to diminish its value but merely to emphasize that in terms of music's role within the black community, the shift to jazz as *art music* was a move away from the community's oral roots toward the embracing of literate values. This is apparent in many ways. Bebop emphasized complex harmonic theory based on literate principles of musical structure; it stressed individual expression over the articulation of the needs of the community. Bebop abandoned dance, shifting its emphasis from the body to the mind; bebop gave up its role as a social lubricant and retreated to the literate garret; bebop (with the exception of Dizzy's loveable clowning) abandoned the rituals of showbiz, of public invitation. For most people, jazz was no longer party music, no longer fucking music, no longer good-time music. Jazz seemed to have lost its sense of humour, its earthiness, its popularity.

For those willing to follow Bird and Diz and Miles and Monk, however, the rewards were sublime. Because they hadn't really abandoned their roots. They remained poets of the first order, lucid elocutionists of epic range and passion. Narrators of mythic histories and prophets of future magic. For those with ears to hear, there was no little humour in Bird's ornithological arabesques, no little seductive fire in Miles's sculpted caresses. But it took work, and it didn't feel like much of a party.

The party was elsewhere, far from art, far from literate culture, far from white folks, farther and farther from jazz. The party was kinetic, sexy, funny, electric. The party was oral. The party was where blacks were dancing to Louis Jordan and his Tympani Five pumping out popular "jump blues" numbers like "Caledonia," "Saturday Night Fish Fry," "Is You Is or Is You Ain't My Baby," and "Beans and Cornbread" (featuring a hilarious gastronomic sermon by a leather-lunged vocalist who would later change his name to Malcolm X). The party was calling into existence R & B. The party was making way for a new black pop music.

If bebop took the mind and ran, elevating its adepts from entertainers to intellectuals, R & B gladly reclaimed the body, dedicating itself to getting down. R & B worked the funny bone, the lips, the stiff prick, the skin, the hair, the tingling muscle. It worked the swinging hip, the lift, the flip, the twirl. It kicked off shoes, undid brassieres, threw punches, shed tears. R & B was the funkified, urbanized, electric blues, the boogie-woogie, honey-dripping blues, the updated, signifying blues. It was the backsliding preacher shaking his tail feathers; it was the devil himself on the dance floor cutting a rug. It was on jukeboxes, on black radio, and at theatres across America. It was ladies on top, with the likes of Laverne Baker, Ruth Brown, Etta James, and Big Maybelle. It was loud. And once again, most white folks hated and feared it; demonizing the boogying black body even more than the bebopping black mind.

To mutate in the middle, rock 'n' roll is *black and tan* music. It's music made by white boys in love with black music, rooted in R & B but recast with hillbilly or Liverpudlian accents. It's the unashamed appropriation of popular black music by white kids who grew up surrounded by it or gravitated toward it as rebellious teenagers. Elvis Presley's first hit record was a cover of Big Daddy Crudup's "It's All Right." Elvis captured the hearts and loins of white American youth with words and music borrowed from black America. His eye-popping moves were borrowed too, mostly from Jackie Wilson. And the same thing kept happening as rock 'n' roll grew more and more popular. The black songwriter Otis Blackwell supplied Elvis with hits such as "Don't Be Cruel," "Return to Sender," and "All Shook Up." He supplied Jerry Lee Lewis with "Great Balls of Fire," and the world with the immortal, immaculate "Fever." Bill Haley and the Comets recorded Sunny Dae's 1952 hit, "Rock Around the Clock" in 1954, the same year they struck gold with Big Joe Turner's "Shake, Rattle and Roll." And why not? They were good songs and good lyrics. Hardworking lyrics. American lyrics. They were variations on the long-suffering, well-worn poetry of the blues. And besides, it wasn't words white kids were after. They had words shoved down their throats every day at school, at home, at work. And they never meant anything, those hypocritical words, about marks, manners, morals, traditions, careers. The kids weren't looking for more words. The kids were looking for their bodies. And they found them, dancing to rock 'n' roll.

Dancing to rock 'n' roll changed everything. Suddenly, white kids felt alive. They moved, they sweated. Suddenly, the walls were shaking, skirts were flying, people were jumping up and down. Even if you couldn't jitterbug, you could still shake, rattle, and roll. You could still do the Twist or the Frug. You could dance to black music, feel the thrill of doing something transgressive, something risqué, something explicitly sexual. But most of all, you could taste something real, something deep, something that felt like freedom. The words meant nothing. The experience was everything. The physical sensation, the emotional intensity, the devotion to the moment — rock 'n' roll opened the door to a new world of possibilities that instantly made an enemy of the bland conformity of white 50s America.

The same thing had happened before in the late 20s. Then, as in the 50s, a generation of American youth embraced black music as the key to its liberation from rigid moral codes. The flappers and their peers danced to jazz like there was no tomorrow, doing ancient African dance steps that they knew as the Charleston, certain that the future was theirs. Women would step into the expanding workforce and the mainstream of society. Victorian ideas about sex and propriety would wither away forever. There were good times ahead in America!

But the moment failed, done in by the Great Depression. Thirty years later, however, as a new generation of youth embraced black music with hormones raging, each new year brought only greater prosperity. And there were many more teenagers in the 50s than in the 20s, more than there had ever been before perhaps. And technology was in play now too, with radios in every white middle-class bedroom, quietly piping The Moonglows and the Soul Stirrers and Little Richard in the secret teenage blackness of the midwestern night. This time there would be no collapse. This time women would not be thrust back. This time black folks were making their own push for social revolution. This time would be different.

It was the rehabilitation of the body that young white America longed for. And by the early 60s it was at hand. The Beatles made it clear to the remaining skeptics when they touched down in America in 1964 amid teenage chaos that there was no turning back. As they landed, the words of an American singer serenaded them:

Come mothers and fathers throughout the land
And don't criticize what you can't understand
Your sons and your daughters are beyond your command
Your old road is rapidly aging
So get out of the new one if you can't lend a hand
for the times they are a changing[59]

Bob Dylan is the symbolic nexus, and to some degree the catalyst that would allow rock 'n' roll to become more, much more, than a horny teenage fad. Because Dylan showed white rock 'n' rollers that contrary to what they had thought, *words did matter;* that to make their way as oral poets they had a lot more work to do; but above all that they were fully equipped with the tools needed to reinvent their world.

Blues lyrics — as poetically potent and socially subversive as they were — were borrowed from blacks. They belonged to black Americans. They were the expression of black experience. Ultimately, although white American and British kids related to the alienation, the suffering, and the defiance of the blues, these words were not theirs. Borrowing the music made sense because the music was the body, and it was the body that white kids craved. But borrowing the words was a temporary necessity, a stop-gap until someone figured out how to integrate the gift of the body with the legacy of a vast, syncretic language of poetry and power.

Dylan made it clear that there was nothing about which kids could not sing. He unleashed the full vocabulary of the English language on rock 'n' roll. He cajoled the visionary poetic angel into flight and sang its praises. He introduced explicitly political songs, protest songs whose form he had learned from Woody Guthrie and his forbears, but whose articulation was his alone, and that of his generation. White kids were given back their bodies by black music but they were returned their subconscious by Dylan. When Dylan sang "The answer is blowin' in the wind" it was an invitation to find answers within oneself, to seek out the rustling winds of emotion blowing in one's soul and to listen to the truths they bore. Dylan wrote "Blowin' in the Wind" in 1962. Two years later it was recorded by fourteen year-old Stevie Wonder. And although Berry Gordy resisted, Little Stevie insisted. Even at fourteen he knew the score. This was a song that questioned the soul of a nation. Dylan's best songs — like those of all great popular poets — are wells sunk deep into the soul, wells that both relieve private pressure and release public power.

Dylan signalled the triumph of oral poetry for white America, the reconciliation of the word and the body, of the singer and the song, of the poet and the community. From here on in, it was a party.

Suddenly, the body belonged to white America as it had always belonged to black America. And now that it had been reunited with the word, tongues began wagging, stories started spilling forth, and spirits began churning. Just as Mezzrow had heard the south side of Chicago transformed in the 20s by the electric language of liberty, so did the 60s resound with the dancing poetry of the moment, a poetry of celebration, of defiance, of dreams.

17 Word and Deed

AFTER 1964, the simplistic and derivative rock 'n' roll lyrics of young white artists suddenly blossomed into a vast garden of poetic delights. Among many others, John Lennon, Paul McCartney, Lou Reed, Neil Young, Jim Morrison, Steven Stills, Van Morrison, Mick Jagger, Roger McGuinn, Frank Zappa, Ed Sanders, and Tuli Kupferberg wrote songs with lyrics that were resoundingly fresh, the best of which resembled nothing heard before. "Good or bad, who's to say, but original is definitely what we were," says Jefferson Airplane's Grace Slick, recalling what she describes as "the seemingly overnight changes in lyrics."[60]

During that same period, there was an equally abundant blossoming of black music. Indie labels like Stax, King, VeeJay, and Motown churned out hit after monster hit performed by the likes of The Temptations, The Supremes, Aretha Franklin, Marvin Gaye, Little Stevie Wonder, James Brown, Otis Redding, Wilson Pickett, and Smokey Robinson — and they are just part of the remarkable pool of black performing talent on the scene in the 60s. But what about the songs themselves? And what about their lyrics? Did they too undergo a "seemingly overnight change" as had white pop-music lyrics?

One strand of our story has been the increasingly sensitive, ambitious, and celebratory responses of white Americans — especially poets

— to black music during the twentieth century. As we have seen, black music made possible the reconciliation of the white body with the white word in America in the 60s, and Bob Dylan announced its arrival. But what of the other strand — the strand that represents blacks and their search for an equally potent reconciliation, a reconciliation of word and body, of word and deed? If the 60s witnessed the blossoming of one of those two interwoven strands, might it not have yielded the triumph of the other? Can we not point to an individual and say here, in the voice of this black man or woman, at this turning point in the history of black America, mirroring the resurgence of a victorious white body-music, we find at last the resurgence of an unbounded black word-language — of the empowered, embodied voice that makes way for a generation, liberating minds and spirits with a poetic flow of unprecedented potency, in the right place at the right time with the humble prophetic tongue afire?

Maybe. In a sense this question is at the heart of this book. I'm telling history as a pair of symbiotic stories, and one of my stories has just reached a climax. One of my stories is — for now — complete. Narrative symmetry dictates that the second story should also now reach its historical conclusion. It makes sense that if the reconciliation of the white body and word happened in the midst of — and as an essential part of — an extraordinary American social upheaval in the 60s, that the reconciliation of the black word and body should have happened at the same time, as an equally essential part of an equally extraordinary and contemporaneous black American social upheaval. Doesn't it? Or does it?

Our starting point in the search for the liberated black word must be within the civil rights movement. What was the status of black music and of black poetry within the movement? In Pete Seeger and Bob Reiser's *Everybody Says Freedom: A History of the Civil Rights Movement in Songs and Pictures*, music's importance to the movement was remembered by prominent activists:

> There was music in everything we did. If you had a staff meeting, or if you were just hanging around the office, somebody would just come out with a song. Or if there were bad feeling, a painful discussion, tension, anybody, not a singer or anything, just anybody at the meeting or in the office, would open up with a line

of a song, and somebody else would take it over, and somebody else would add a verse, and by the end, everybody would be hugging each other and loving each other.

(CORDELL REAGON)[61]

After our first meetings I realized how much those songs I had learned, those freedom songs, could help pull us together. It was an organizational glue. I asked people to think about a song they might sing that night and then change that song. Think about freedom, interject your own feelings, your own words ... Out of that came freedom songs we'd be singing all across Mississippi.

(SAM BLOCK)[62]

Some of those night marches were unbelievable. They had this central square. And we'd march around the square. I remember this one night. The white mob was around the entire square. But it was clustered most strongly on this one side of the square where the real Klan leaders were ... We were singing. Somehow, I can't explain it, through the singing and the sense of our solidarity we made a kind of psychological barrier between us and the mob ... It wasn't visual, but you could almost see our singing and our unity pushing them back ... Eventually the only way they could get through was to bombard us with rocks.

(BRUCE HARTFORD)[63]

There was a woman at Shiloh Baptist Church who could sing one song for an hour. It is not a song anymore. People are clapping, feet are going, you can hear her three blocks away. Your ears are not enough, your eyes are not enough, your body is not enough. The only way to survive the singing is to open up and let go and be moved by it to another place ... The voice I have now I got ... after I got out of jail, I did the song "Over My Head I See Freedom in the Air," but I had never heard that voice before. I had never been that me before ... A transformation had taken place in all of us.

(BERNICE JOHNSON REAGON)[64]

The songs of the civil rights movement constituted a return to a condition of near-pure orality. Singing played an essential role in the movement, or rather a multitude of roles, all directly tied to the communalizing and transformative capacity of song. But how important were the words in these songs? On the one hand, not very important at all. In the words of Bernice Johnson Reagon (who was co-founder of the SNCC Freedom Singers in 1962 and went on to found the Grammy award-winning Sweet Honey in the Rock) speaking of those civil rights songs, "See it's not about words, it's about spirit."[65] And in the context of building and maintaining a sense of community, this is clearly true. Yet the civil rights songs served a second, equally important purpose: they sent a message to the outside world, and words were an important part of that message. That "We Shall Overcome" became the movement's anthem is no accident. It is a bold, unforgiving, and defiant statement of revolutionary faith articulated in language — and therefore profoundly subversive of the status quo. The violent Klansmen surrounding that town square may have been disarmed equally by the explicit articulation of black resistance in words — something they had never imagined — as by the powerful magic of collective song.

And yet these songs — and their potent lyrics — cannot be said to have achieved a lasting redemption of language for black America. Inextricably linked, as they are, to a specific historical context, one in which the transformative strength of black America's oral heritage was made manifest, they represent a stage, yet another stepping stone on the path to a fully empowered black word-language.

In the late 50s and early 60s, the music of avant-garde "free" jazz musicians like Ornette Coleman, Albert Ayler, Archie Shepp, Cecil Taylor, and Eric Dolphy constituted a sophisticated and confrontational articulation of the complex challenge posed by black culture to white America. Despite the quality of these achievements, we find only a modest impact on the popular black discourse when we gauge their wider influence. Most of these artists knowingly sought their sophisticated articulation at the expense of an unsophisticated audience. Jazz was no longer popular music, at least not the kind played by the likes of Albert Ayler or Cecil Taylor. Free jazz is reminiscent of the hoodoo worshippers hiding in the shadows silently mouthing their ecstatic prayers. That is to say, Dolphy and Shepp and Coleman were speaking the truth, but they were testifying in relative isolation, their voices ignored by the larger community. Meanwhile, the public voices still rooted in the church, the hit-making, gospel-influenced, soul-singing voices, retained their oral power but were not permitted complete freedom of language. As before, one could have the true word without a voice (or in this case an audience, which for an oralist is almost the same thing) or the true voice without words.

Despite the rising tide of political activism in black America and the increasingly violent racial conflicts captivating the nation, in the late 50s and early 60s black artists produced very few explicitly political R & B songs. In fact, as Brian Ward says in his insightful book, *Just My Soul Responding: Rhythm and Blues, Black Consciousness and Race Relations*, "although there were some exceptions, soul — like R & B, rock and roll, and black pop before it — had become the premiere musical expression of mass black consciousness in the early-to-mid 1960s while paying relatively little explicit attention to the ongoing freedom struggle."[66]

Systemic racism within the music industry was a major stumbling block. All of the major record labels and most of the independent ones were owned by whites. Similarly, almost all of the radio stations were owned by whites. And without airplay, artists had almost no chance of reaching a substantial audience. Although a number of indie record labels were owned by blacks who might conceivably have been interested in releasing lyrically challenging songs if they had had hit potential, such songs would have had little chance of getting radio airplay. Black labels depended on a relationship with commercial radio, in which it was understood that "stirring up trouble" would result in severe penalties. This in turn resulted in a highly effective form of self-censorship. Those who transgressed the code paid a price. When James Brown released his furiously funky and bigot-frightening "Say It Loud, I'm Black and I'm Proud" in 1968, it proved to be his last appearance on the R & B charts for seventeen years. J. B. said it loud, said it proud, and wasn't heard again on the radio for a long, long time.

But it was not only the political conservatism of the white-dominated music industry that held black artists back. The black pop-music formula was too successful for its own good. Although the assembly-line model, which isolated songwriters from performers from producers, worked magnificently in uniting the strengths and skills of creative individuals, this process ultimately stifled the development of independent black voices and unconventional songs. Having written and produced dozens of hit songs, producer teams like Ashford and Simpson, Holland-Dozier-Holland, and Bristol and Fuqua were far more powerful than most performers, and they stuck to their proven winning formulas, leaving little opportunity for black singers to grow into mature independent artists. Above all, it meant artists and labels were constantly minimizing rather than encouraging creative risk-taking.

Another reason for the inability of R & B and early soul music to explicitly articulate the struggles being fought by blacks in America at that time may be the nature and power of black orality itself. In his 1964 review of LeRoi Jones's *Blues People*, Ralph Ellison argues that "the blues, the spirituals, the jazz, the dance — was what we had in place of freedom . . . the blues are not primarily concerned with civil rights; they are an art form and thus a transcendence of those conditions created within the Negro community by the denial of social justice."[67]

Ellison's argument — that art is a transcendence of unjust social conditions as opposed to a direct attack upon them — is particularly apt with regard to the blues, of which R & B and soul music are extensions. We have seen how black music served as a means of asserting both community and identity for blacks in America from slavery onward. Music was a means of embodying freedom in what Hakim Bey has called a *temporary autonomous zone*. In singing the blues, in listening to the blues, the freedom to be in the moment is made manifest. Thus, as is typical of an oral culture, the communication event becomes an end in itself. Its essence lies not in referring to or acting on outside forces, but in experiencing the present with those present. Thus, if blacks "had music in place of freedom," it would make sense that in the face of an unprecedented struggle for social freedom, there would exist a tension between the traditional "escape" and the realm of social action. Perhaps black popular music — never intended to inspire action but rather to provide an alternative, affirmative universe given the impossibility of action — inherently resisted the imposition of "serious" ends and an enforced reference to external realities beyond the confines of the temporary autonomous zone.

Still another explanation lies in the historic centrality of indirection to the black poetic aesthetic. How difficult it must have been and how strange it must have felt for black singers who had mastered a metaphorical idiom to try to explicitly name the enemy, to trace its shape in hard edges rather than fluid suggestion. This cultural dilemma is particularly apparent when contrasted to the songs of disenfranchised working-class white youth in England in the mid-60s, whose cultural gift for articulating seething anger and raw scorn may be unmatched in the world. Nothing in the 60s soul music canon compares for example, to The Who's "My Generation," in which Roger Daltrey sneeringly stutters out lines like "Why don't you all just f-f-f-ade away" and "Hope I die before I get old."

Due to these several factors — the resistance of white-controlled radio, the timidity of black labels, the economic dependencies of artists, black music's function as an "alternative reality," and the tradition of black indirection — black lyrics remained largely aloof from the civil rights movement during its bitterest struggles and greatest triumphs. In February 1965, however, just fourteen months after it had been retired, the R & B chart was reinstated in *Billboard.* Black and white tastes were again veering sharply apart as the desire to express and affirm essentialist "blackness" began shaping popular black consciousness.

By the mid-60s, the optimism that had characterized the early civil rights movement began to wane. The language of non-violence was no longer satisfactory to an increasing number of blacks who felt that what little change was occurring was happening far too slowly. They demanded a more assertive word-language. "I ain't about to be non-violent, honey," sang Nina Simone in her pugnacious song "Mississippi Goddam." As aggressively confrontational cultural and political strategies gained currency among American blacks, as leaders were murdered and churches were bombed, soul music lyrics swung toward a more explicit articulation of black identity and black struggle. When Aretha Franklin's version of Otis Redding's "Respect" topped the charts in 1967, it signaled to black artists and white record-label owners alike that black songs could be commercially successful despite — or indeed because of — their political content. What followed was a steady stream of politically expressive songs by the likes of Sly Stone ("Don't Call Me Nigger, Whitey, There's a Riot Going On"), The Staple Singers ("Respect Yourself"), The Temptations ("Ball of Confusion"), Edwin Starr ("War"), and eventually the spangled interstellar funkster George

Clinton ("America Eats Its Young"). Even the musically conservative Smokey Robinson, who had for so long helped steer the Motown ship of state clear of the troublesome shoals of political engagement, finally recognized the need for black music to respond to the transformative events and ideas that were shaping black experience.

For generations, black musicians — including black vocalists — had performed for white audiences, or with the awareness of a secondary white audience beyond the primary black audience, but never before had black lyrics addressed white America from an explicitly racialized position or from a position of equality. Nor had black lyrics explicitly challenged blacks to refine and redefine their relationships with whites as part of redefining their relationship with themselves, as did Curtis Mayfield in one of the most lyrically provocative — and deliciously tuneful — songs of his day, "Choice of Colors":

If you had a choice, my brother
Which one would you choose, my brother?
If there was no day or night
Which one would you prefer to be right?[68]

Remarkably few songs by black artists addressed social issues with Mayfield's sensitivity. James Brown's "Say It Loud, I'm Black and I'm Proud" was a necessary assertion of personal revolution, an affirmation never before articulated, and as such it deserves enormous respect. And yet, beyond this powerful slogan, a universe of possibilities remained unspoken, so much so that what may be the most potent political articulation of black consciousness in music in the 60s — Jimi Hendrix's passionate mangling of the "Star Spangled Banner" at Woodstock — is a recapitulation of the historic wordlessness so familiar to black America. Hendrix's gut-wrenching fusillade is aimed directly at the flag, but he's shooting — not blanks exactly — but bloody kisses, question marks, himself. His assertion of defiance was a martyrdom. His faith in transcendent oral creativity was heretical in a literate world.

In early 1971, just months after Hendrix's untimely death, Motown released Marvin Gaye's self-produced LP *What's Going On*. It was the first time that a major black artist was given the power to shape his own music and write his own lyrics without bowing to the dominant sounds of the day. Motown kingpin Berry Gordy had resisted Gaye's attempt to wrest creative control of his music away from the hit-making machine and to focus on the artistic value of the "concept album" rather than the economic value of the hit single. But finally, with Motown's Smokey Robinson convinced Gaye's pet project was "the greatest album ever made," *What's Going On* was released. It was an instant classic, generating massive acclaim and stunning sales.

On the album's title track, Gaye assumes the role of a black soldier just back from Vietnam, trying with difficulty to understand the changes that have taken place at home since he went to war. His sense of confusion works on many levels, engaging listeners in a heartfelt search for meaning and challenging them to take stock of the scope and significance of ongoing social changes. The uncertainty Gaye's character feels allowed blacks pushing for social justice to acknowledge the strangeness and scariness of engaging in such a momentous and subversive uprising. That same expression of vulnerability may also have allowed whites to feel a sense of relief as they too struggled to understand what was going on. Gaye's ingenious humility opens the door for all Americans to sit back and ponder the tenor of the times. In so doing, Gaye implicitly suggests, they will realize that what's going on is the collective search for justice, decency, and love.

Once Marvin Gaye opened the door, Stevie Wonder followed him through, first gaining creative and economic control of his work from Motown, and then creating several of the most enduring and ambitious albums of the 70s, including the legendary *Innervisions*, *Talking Book*, and *Songs in the Key of Life*. More than any other black singers of this era, Stevie Wonder and Marvin Gaye managed to fuse and express a profound commitment to black self-determination and a joyous cultural celebration with incisive social commentary and a deeply personal expression of collective feeling. They successfully transmuted generations of suffering into compassionate affirmations of possibility, permitting millions of black Americans to unload some of that pain and replace it with hope, pride, and determination. They reclaimed their oral heritage as community leaders with vision and unmatched skill.

And yet, on the ground, in the streets, things were still not changing fast enough. As the heat was turned up from year to year in the late 60s, as black America's repressed aggression was inflamed — by ever more shameless racist provocation and by the looming possibility of victory or, at least, revenge — a turning point came. Enraged by white resistance to meaningful change at the local level, deprived by murderous hate of popular leaders equal to the task of redirecting a people's rising anger toward constructive ends, of sinking wells sturdy enough to handle the gushers of black anger, the black subconscious remained stifled. And then, in Watts, in Detroit, in Chicago, summer after summer, it blew. The result was urban violence and rioting on a scale not seen in America since the civil war.

But when the burning and looting stopped, the pain remained. The anger remained. The black subconscious had not been healed, merely momentarily purged. Time passed. Although important and lasting social gains had been achieved, the floodgates did not open. Not the floodgates of prosperity. Not the floodgates of equality. Not the floodgates of truth. White America opened its heart — a crack — then stopped. Instead of equality, it offered black America more poverty, more unemployment, and continuing discrimination. It offered crack cocaine to the ghetto, and the soulless consumerism of suburbia to those who managed to escape the ghetto's bleak confines.

Significantly, two of the greatest comedic voices of black America (comedians, like poets, are subversive and catalytic oralists unlocking repressed emotions), Bill Cosby and Richard Pryor, succumbed spectacularly to these twin evils. Each had incisively attacked the prejudices of white America and challenged black America to see itself without shame or self-deception. By the early 80s, however, TV star Bill Cosby was the poster boy for Hollywood's brand-name American Dream, an illusory universe in which blackness had been bleached and infinite affluence (both on- and offscreen) was the norm. Meanwhile, Richard Pryor, after emptying a shotgun into his wife's car, had incinerated his mind and body with etherized coke, a poster child for self-destruction.

The "soul revolution" was a proud step toward the redemption of African orality. Voices were heard expressing emotions, ideas, and dreams that needed to be expressed. Communities were united in song, given strength in song, gained self-knowledge in song. To some degree, oral emancipation resulted in literate change. Laws were rewritten as a result of putting singing bodies in the way of clubs, cannons, and dogs. Policies were enacted in the wake of historic speeches that seared a nation's soul. Yet there were signs that the emerging redemption of orality, though culturally and politically significant, was inadequate to topple the literate hegemony. The printed word continued to shackle black America in its collective effort to claim its rightful share of American economic and political power.

18 Black Poets on the Page

Our music has always been the most dominant manifestation of what we are and feel; literature was just an afterthought, the step taken by the Negro bourgeoisie who desired acceptance on the white man's terms. And that is precisely why the literature has failed. It was the case of one elite addressing another elite.

But our music is something else. The best of it has always operated at the core of our lives, forcing itself upon us as in a ritual. It has always, somehow, represented the collective psyche. Black Literature must attempt to achieve that same sense of the collective ritual.[69]

—LARRY NEAL (1968)

The poetry I want to write is oral by tradition, mass aimed as its fundamental functional motive.[70]

— AMIRI BARAKA (1987)

In their insistence upon jazz as a model and inspiration, these writers were and are confronted with enormous technical problems, some of which may be insoluble if they continue to write that poetry down. For their model is dynamic not static ... The central problem is the printed page.[71]

—STEPHEN E. HENDERSON (1972)

In 1970 the challenge was — and is — clear for black America: make black writing as expressive, as transformative, as representative of the collective psyche, as black music; infuse the page with the vitality of orality; create a liberating, popular black literature. But has that challenge been met? Did black America acquire an authentic word-language by embracing — and then subverting — the hegemony of print? Is black literature as potent as black music?

In 1970, Ishmael Reed understood better than anyone the problems that would confront black writers seeking to meet these challenges. He had already published two formally and idiomatically inventive novels, *The Freelance Pallbearers* (1967) and *Yellow Back Radio Broke Down* (1969), when in 1972, in an adventurous exploration of what would eventually be known as postmodern self-referentiality, he made the search for a culturally representative black literature his subject matter in a novel called *Mumbo Jumbo*. In this year Reed also published his "Neo-HooDoo Manifesto," in which he articulated his belief in a magical practice of creative invention — based on African traditions but informed by the ideas and spirituality of all of the peoples of the New World — that had been exiled from America at the dawn of modernity but was at last returning to conjure up a contemporary black culture of transformative power. And although Reed — as an author, a literate — does not locate the strength of Neo-HooDoo exclusively in its oral roots, he nonetheless pays homage to those roots while arguing that a fully realized black word-language can only be achieved by transmuting the power of orality into textuality:

> Neo-HooDoo is a litany seeking its text
> Neo-HooDoo is a Dance and Music closing in on its words
> Neo-HooDoo is a Church finding its lyrics
> Cecil Brown Al Young Calvin Hernton
> David Henderson Steve Cannon Quincy Troupe
> Ted Joans Victor Cruz N.H. Pritchard Ishmael Reed
> Lennox Raphael Sarah Fabio Ron Welburn are Neo
> HooDoo's "Manhattan Project" of writing.[72]

Although Reed expresses faith in the possibility of this transmutation, he also recognizes it implies an essential incongruity that must be overcome. *Mumbo Jumbo* is an explicit — albeit subtle and structurally complex — articulation of this difficult paradox: how can an oralist embrace literacy without sacrificing oral values? *Mumbo Jumbo* is thus a crash course in the collision of oral and literate values in black America.

Mumbo Jumbo is a parody, a sermon, a mythology, a detective story, a shadow history, an argument, and a conjurer's charm. It is a gumbo of esoterica and arcana strained from cultures as diverse as Pharaonic Egypt, Hollywood, and AfroAmerica. It uses a vast array of inventive textual interstitials — a partial bibliography, multiple narratives, bits of texts from disparate sources woven in and out — to accentuate the subject matter, which is the nature of black textuality. The book's central character, named Jes Grew, is not a person at all, but rather the personification of the Neo-HooDoo life force, equivalent to Lorca's *duende* or Taoist *chi.* The character's name is derived from a phrase used by James Weldon Johnson, the celebrated Harlem Renaissance poet, preacher, and author, to refer to the manner of composition of ragtime tunes. Where did they come from? "They *jes' grew.*" Reed, recognizing the deeper undercurrents of creative blackness, turns Jes Grew into the essence of Neo-HooDoo power. *Mumbo Jumbo* revolves around the search by Pa Pa La Bas for Jes Grew's long-lost sacred text. Throughout the novel, Jes Grew never speaks. *Jes Grew is wordless.*

In *Mumbo Jumbo*, Reed gives his interpretation of one of the two interwoven tales I have told in this book: the search for black words. Rather than simply explaining it, he offers — he enacts — a solution. Reed's solution is manifest at the book's climax, leading up to which Pa Pa La Bas recites an esoteric history of the ancient myth of Thoth and his gift of writing to the Egyptians, before drawing a complex lineage from that first African book to Jes Grew's lost sacred text. When the ornate and mysterious box containing the sacred text is finally produced and opened before a breathless gathering, to everyone's surprise and dismay the box is empty. There is no book. There is no sacred text.

Does this mean Jes Grew is doomed to wordlessness? On the contrary, Ishmael Reed has himself conjured Jes Grew's text into existence. *Mumbo Jumbo* — an extraordinary poetic recapitulation of African-American consciousness — is itself the lost book that rehabilitates the magical tradition of black words. And yet, as the empty box makes clear, Jes Grew's text also does not exist, can never exist, *because it cannot be fixed but must always be recreated.* It is this continual recreation reflecting each individual imagination and voice that is the essence of Jes Grew and of Neo-HooDoo, and which Reed posits as a force capable of transcending oppression. This is Reed's authentic sorcery: he brings black folks to the edge of self-realization and then hurls them over the edge, standing behind on the cliffside waving. *Yes, this is the truth. Now don't follow me, follow yourself!*

And so, thirty years after Ishmael Reed, Larry Neal, and others first articulated the challenge facing black writers, it's time to ask: has black writing become as potent as black music? Is it imbued with the energy of orality? Has the book embraced the body?

Although one can point to individual black American authors, especially women, who have remade writing in their image — who have created potent black literary idioms and transcendent poetic works — the cultural significance of black literature remains dwarfed by that of black music in black America today.

Black literature has not been able to overcome the fundamental paradox of its stated mission. Black writers have not, despite their achievements, succeeded in making black literature as fluid, as emotive, as "oral" as black music. How could they? The two media are not just profoundly different from one another, but the values each embodies are fiercely antagonistic. Lyrics can be transcribed; typographic conventions and artistry can imply conversational dynamics; repetition, rhyme, and implied rhythm in writing can imply music; stories can be written about storytellers and oral traditions; but even at its best, literature can never approximate the experience of orality, of black music. Not because orality is "better" but because its essence lies in qualities that cannot be crammed into a book, and cannot coexist with the experience of textuality. You can't write and talk at the same time. Or read and listen.

Ishmael Reed's faith in the ability of black literature to constantly reinvent itself, to become an ongoing spiritual revolution — as black music has always done and been — is misguided. Reed mistakenly assumes that his achievement — that of enacting a black textual revolution — can be repeated by others, few of whom share his talent or vision. Moreover, he fails to recognize the pitfalls of literacy and the profound resistance to the essence of Jes Grew that is endemic to the literate mindset. Reed argues that literature can be transformed into a medium that privileges process over product, improvisation over reproduction, the creative impulse over the residual artifact. But he has fooled himself.

He has bought into his own conjurer's illusion. *Reed believes that black writers can make books disappear.* But they can't.

Literacy is addictive, because it is empowering. But literacy always demands specific material, intellectual, and economic responses. It is inherently exegetical. Despite Reed's warning not to fix the black text, his novels are now being taught in thousands of English and African-American literature classes across America. Moreover, there is an emerging black literature canon; a postmodern black literature critical apparatus; black lit lectures, award ceremonies, textbooks, panel discussions, degrees, colloquia, and all the rest. It is the inevitable byproduct of a literate culture.

Despite the tremendous poetic and social value of black literature, it suffers from the same inherent limitations that drove white poets to black music in the first place. Although the embracing of literate values by a minority of black Americans has resulted in access to the (previously segregated) language of political, economic, and intellectual power in America, it has not resulted in a socio-poetic reconciliation of the word and the body. Rather, it has been a catalyst of the growing schism between a black middle class that has mastered the levers of literate power — legal contracts, SATs, business reports, government forms, and so on — and been assimilated into literate capitalism, and a disenfranchised black majority that continues to cling to devalued oral ideals and modalities.

19 Black Poets on the Stage

MANY BLACK WRITERS grappling with the paradox of black textuality have collaborated with musicians to bridge the divide between page and stage. As noted earlier with reference to the beats, poets and jazz musicians worked together regularly in the late 50s. Yet long before the beats did it, Langston Hughes, among the first modern black poets to have unabashedly celebrated blackness in America, was working with jazz musicians.

In 1958, in the midst of the jazz and poetry fad, Hughes recorded an album titled *The Weary Blues*, on which he is accompanied by two very different jazz bands. Side A sees him in the company of men in their forties and fifties, men who have lived the history of jazz: trumpeter Red Allen, trombonist Vic Dickenson, bassist Milt Hinton, drummer Osie Johnson, pianist Al Williams, and saxophonist Sam "The Man" Taylor. The group treats Langston Hughes and his spoken words as they would a bluesman. They sit back and allow the singer to sing; the preacher to preach; the speaker to speak. With the confidence that comes from decades of listening and playing, the ensemble supports, embellishes, and expands on Hughes's lyrics at every turn, yet never intrudes on his spotlight. On the A side of this record, the fusion of poetry and music is relaxed and successful.

On the B side, Langston Hughes is accompanied by a group of younger men — bassist Charles Mingus, pianist Horace Parlan, saxman Shafi Hadi, trombonist Jimmy Knepper, and drummer Kenny Dennis — all in their twenties and thirties. This ensemble treats Hughes as a poet; a poet whose work they respect, whose words are perhaps musical, but whose role in their ensemble is unclear. The quintet performs hesitantly, only achieving the fluid intensity that was otherwise their hallmark when Hughes stops reciting. There is no place in their music for a poet, and on the B side of *The Weary Blues*, despite the best of intentions, the union of poetry and music is an aesthetic failure.

Unlike the musicians with whom Hughes recorded, whose creative language was rarely self-conscious, Hughes's poetry was intensely self-conscious. For Hughes to speak out in defence of his world, he had to fracture the totality of its underlying principles. He had to isolate poetry from music, the creative event from the community, the poem from the voice. His search for a poetic language that would accurately reflect and passionately speak to the everyday experiences of his peers inevitably led him to this paradox: that the poetry he sought already existed. It was flourishing all about him, and by trying to capture it in "poetry" (that is to say, *written* poetry), he would of necessity be betraying it. And yet by temperament he was a writer, not a singer. And he could not remain silent. He had to celebrate — and mourn — his world. He chose to speak out. Or, more accurately, he chose to write.

Hughes had to suffer the limitations of his choice. He didn't sing the blues. Instead, he wrote them and then read them. His speaking voice is rich and warm, full of playful ironies and gentle urgings, and yet it cannot match the voice of Sam "The Man" Taylor for expressiveness. Or that of Joe Turner, Joe Williams, or Jimmy Rushing. Abstracted from song, stripped of melody, his lyrics seem awkward and out of place. Hughes can only imply rather than embody their magical potency. On *The Weary Blues*, Hughes is a black man shaped primarily by orality reciting literate poems inspired by black orality in the company of oral poets performing *their* poems musically. Wow! All of the poets are tremendously skilled, and the ultimate aims of their communications are so intertwined, that these labyrinthine levels of historical evolution are easily transcended, allowing the ensemble to seamlessly give the poet's words a meaningful life in sound. The band on side A makes

Hughes an honorary bluesman, and he responds with all the knowledge of his life in poetry.

Why doesn't the second side — the Mingus side — work as well? To begin with, this band insists on being noticed. The young ego needs space, and the poem can only tolerate so much interference. At times, the musicians get in the way. Although at other times the talent, energy, and intuition of the ensemble produces some stunning interaction, there is an overall lack of direction and definition. The second stumbling block is rhythm. The Red Allen band swings low and easy, slow and steady. Even when the tempo increases, the band retains its relaxed feel. The Mingus group is far more adventurous with respect to rhythm, and as a result the tempos and accents often shift; sometimes subtly, sometimes abruptly. Most likely in response to this shifting, Hughes chose to read poems whose accents and rhythms also meander irregularly. Inevitably, this decision leads to a degree of confusion and uncertainty. It is an unwieldy mixture. Not just because Langston Hughes was unable to lead a group of such aggressive temperament, but above all because the band was unable to adapt to the demands of his word-language. Mingus had better results with poetry on later recordings.

The two sides of *The Weary Blues* offer a striking contrast. On one side, Langston Hughes is treated as an oral performer. Although he was caught between the twin poles of orality and literacy, the jazz ensemble's flexibility enabled the poet to satisfy the demands of the oral role. On the other side, Hughes is treated as a literary poet, and like all writers and readers of poetry, when placed in a jazz context, he is out of place. There is no role for a writer, even a writer as black and as jazzy as Langston Hughes, in jazz music.

The only way for a writer to interact successfully with a band is to become an integral part of the band — to become a musician and a performer — which means abandoning the fixity of textuality in favour of the fluidity of orality. In the history of black word-poetry, several artists have succeeded in making this transition. Amiri Baraka has been among the most determined and adventurous authors to explore this territory. He has recorded tracks with many musicians, including a 1964 performance of his poem "Black Dada Nihilismus" with the New York Art Quartet (Roswell Rudd, John Tchicai, Milford Graves, and Lewis Worrell), released on ESP records. In 1966, Baraka wrote and produced a play, *A Black Mass*, for which Sun Ra's Arkestra supplied the music. This work, along with a later play, *The Dutchman*, are explicit and violent theatrical assaults on white American culture and its racist legacy. They are a mainline into the angry black subconscious that stands in stark contrast to the lyrics of popular black music in the 60s. The short-lived Black Arts Repertory Theater/School, which Baraka founded in 1964, was an explicit attempt to ritualize and publicize black creativity in multiple media, and it was influential in establishing a focus for many younger black artists coming onto the scene. In the ensuing decades, Baraka has continued to be a pivotal figure in both the development of a black literature and the search for a reconciliation of black words and music. He is an arresting poetic performer whose rough and ready voice is capable of embodying idiomatic inspiration and — at his best — inner illumination, though his poems have at times suffered from stylistic rigidity and dogmatism.

Gil Scott-Heron's language is less insistent than Baraka's, and possibly this is why his poems — recited over Brian Jackson's jazz-funk grooves — have proven more popular. When he released his second album, *Pieces of a Man*, in 1972, Scott-Heron established a new benchmark for the fusion of poetry and popular music. His " The Revolution Will Not Be Televised" became an anti-consumerist, anti-media anthem that has only become more relevant in subsequent decades (despite the sad irony of its having been licensed to Nike for pseudo-ironic use in a TV commercial). Scott-Heron was a writer before he became a recording artist, but it is as a poet-performer that he built up a legion of fans around the world. Scott-Heron's poems are eminently accessible due to his casual, everyday vocabulary and delivery and the empathy with which he tackles a range of subjects, some explicitly dealing with problems facing black America and others addressing issues of concern to all people, regardless of their race. The fact that he had a couple of songs that broke into the R & B charts (" The Bottle" hit No. 15 and 1975's "Johannesburg" hit No. 25) — allowed him to continue to release a remarkable fifteen albums between 1972 and 1985. But with little airplay, his success was largely of the fringe variety.

Although he emerged from the fury of the 60s, Scott-Heron is an artist of the 70s and 80s. His politics — radical by mainstream standards — are the politics of human rights. He decries injustice in the 'hood and in South Africa, but he never glosses over the need for each individual black or white person to take responsibility for his or her actions. Gil Scott-Heron has always spoken clearly and insightfully about the black condition in America, expressing — even on that first LP — a rarely heard vulnerability combined with an equally unfamiliar optimism.

When hip hop came of age in the 80s, many critics and even some rappers harkened back to his work as a precursor to their own. At times, Gil Scott-Heron has even been called the grandfather of hip hop, but he dismisses such comparisons. Instead of taking the easy way out and buying into what would no doubt be a lucrative but bogus persona, Scott-Heron chose instead on his 1994 album — with a song called "Message to the Messengers" — to challenge rappers to live up to their own hype:

> hey yeah we're the same brothers from a long time ago
> we was talkin about television and doin it on the radio
> what we did was to help our generation realize
> they got to get out there and get busy cause it wasn't gonna
>   be televised
> see we got respect for young rappers and the way they freewayin'
> but if you goin be teachin folks things be sure you know what
>   you're sayin
> older folks in our neighbourhood got plenty of know how
> remember if it wasn't for them you wouldn't be out there now[73]

Despite his relevance and his talent, despite the fact that he worked in a popular musical idiom and successfully carved out a recording career, despite his moving and potent lyrics, Gil Scott-Heron has never been more than a cult figure. His limitation has not been his own but rather the times he lived in. Whereas Dylan was followed by masses of poets embracing the popular poetry that was rock music, Scott-Heron would not really be followed by anyone. In searching for their roots, hip hoppers would come to know him as a precursor, but Scott-Heron did not influence in any meaningful way the development of hip hop. His work stands the test of time, but in its time it was not fully tested.

Scott-Heron's career parallels to some degree that of The Last Poets, who also have their roots in the 60s and subsequently rose to quasi-prominence as outspoken social critics, activists, and street-corner educators. Formed in 1969 on Malcolm X's birthday, the original ensemble eventually split into two antagonist camps, one led by Jalal Nuruddin and the other by Umar Bin Hassan. At its best, the group has proven extremely potent, skilfully interweaving poetic vocals and relentlessly driving home an intelligent, confrontational agenda in torrents of engaging language and percussive purpose. On their first eponymous LP, which was released in 1970 and gained for the group access to mainstream radio for the first and last time, The Last Poets displayed what would become their characteristic uncompromising intensity on tunes like "Wake Up Niggers," "Niggers Are Scared of Revolution," and "White Man's Got a God Complex" (a line that would later be borrowed by hip-hop legends Public Enemy and turned into a potent track on their 1994 CD *Muse-Sick-and-Hour-Mess-Age*, a.k.a., "music and our message"). Like Gil Scott-Heron, The Last Poets have been adopted as honorary rappers, but with their far sparser and more percussive sound, along with their polyvocal riffing, the group legitimately approximates the rapper's vocal modality far more than Scott-Heron ever did. And given their home in New York City, which is also the home of hip hop, and their many local performances in black neighbourhoods during the 70s, it's fair to suggest that the group influenced many among that first generation of MCs.

Yet another black word-poet to have recorded extensively with musicians is Jayne Cortez. On her six CDs — which feature members of her former husband Ornette Coleman's band, as well as on occasion that august altoist himself — Cortez shows herself to have all of the revolutionary fire possessed by the likes of Amiri Baraka or The Last Poets; the same unquenchable desire for justice, the same febrile anger, the same accusatory intensity. Yet she also possesses the introspective eye and ear, exploring nuances of feeling and experience with a sure and sensual touch; tripping into alternate realities with fluid grace; stretching out sinews and tendons and lips in lonely trust of evanescent truth. In her poetry, Jayne Cortez uses a rich, familiar vocabulary to express complex, familiar feelings in an unaffected voice, which means her poems are accessible to the everyday ear. Yet what goes in through that ear is something profoundly unfamiliar: images and ideas ripped from a relentlessly visceral emotional imagination and served up raw as life.

Is this the redemption of the black word? The reconciliation so long sought after? Yes. Unquestionably. Magnificently. And yet, not quite, not completely. Like the beats before them, Amiri Baraka, Jayne Cortez,

The Last Poets, Gil Scott-Heron, and their kin are precursors of a popular poetic revolution. They set the stage — by *taking* the stage — with a determination to reclaim a black word-language of unbounded grace and power. But the true poetic revolution was still to come.

PART 3

Digitopia

20 Hip Hop's Four Oral Elements

HIP HOP'S FOUR ELEMENTS— rapping, scratching, bombing, and breaking — are a populist avant-garde, heralds of the information age announcing, celebrating, and enacting the neo-oral postliterate cultural experience with an intensity and sophistication that puts the exclusionary theorizing of academic postmodernists to shame. Once again, black music has changed America, this time as a vehicle for black words.

The evolution of rap — but one element of hip hop culture — bears a striking resemblance to the evolution of jazz both stylistically and formally.

The great improvisers of New Orleans jazz (often now referred to as Dixieland jazz) improvised primarily in 2/4 time. Although their playing always swung, it was nonetheless rhythmically regular and highly metrical, as was that of the first great improvisational innovator in jazz, Louis Armstrong. And so too was the rapping of early rap MCs, pioneering poets like Afrika Bambaata, Grandmaster Flash, Grandmaster Caz, Melle Mel, Kurtis Blow, and KRS-1. Although their rapping is speedier and somewhat more syncopated than the pealing riffs of King Oliver or Louis Armstrong, the essential rhythmic pulse is similar. Early rap's 2/4 rhymes typically follow quasi-regular metrical and stanzaic patterns and are anchored firmly by end-rhymes. They were marching rhymes, kick-up-your-feet rhymes, percussive rhymes, jive rhymes.

As jazz evolved, traditional 2/4 stomp-foot time was superseded by a more fluid sense of time. In the mid-30s, Duke Ellington was already pushing the boundaries of jazz rhythms, but the real breakthrough came with bebop drummers like Max Roach, Kenny Clarke, and Art Blakey. They began exploring polyrhythmic nuances previously unimagined in jazz, rethinking and reshaping the rhythmic pulse of "swing" without altering its fundamentally propulsive character. Kenny "Klook" Clarke, for example, became famous for "dropping bombs," which were catalytic bass-drum and cymbal shots dropped into the rhythmic mix at unexpected occasions, a breakthrough that became one of the foundations of modern jazz drumming. Meanwhile the soloists — like pianists Bud Powell, Thelonius Monk, and Herbie Nichols — also abandoned the relaxed character of traditional jazz time and instead began weaving their way electrically in and out of the new asymmetric syncopation, twisting and turning their phrases with greater rhythmic independence and sophistication.

And this development is exactly what happened in hip hop as the first few generations of MCs rapping over post-disco dance beats were superseded by rappers with far greater rhythmic sophistication, rhyming over far more complex and subtle musical beats. The lyrically inventive but angular and relatively predictable phrasing of Kurtis Blow, Melle Mel and Rakim, Kool Moe Dee, Run DMC, and even KRS-1, Ice-T, and LL Cool J gradually gave way to more rhythmically idiosyncratic verbalizing by Tupac, Biggie Smalls, Snoop Doggy Dogg, Too $hort, NWA, and a slew of other thugged-out "gangsta" rappers looking to complement their provocative cultural statements with aesthetic choices that would distance them from rap's party-music origins. No longer were MCs happily hitting downbeats and sticking within the frame of regular 4/4 rhymes. Instead, they slid over and under the beats, breaking phrases without concern for standard musical structure. They abandoned the easy sense of closure provided by the stanzaic form and let poetic form flow organically from lyrical, rhythmic, and narrative impulse. They downplayed the playful exuberance of early rappers and elevated intimidating narrative intimacy as a means of conjuring up an aura of controlled violence. And they began constructing complex dramas in sound, such as NWA's controversial "Fuck Tha Police," which is a classic of the rap radio-play genre.

Formally, rap emerged in part as a localized response to a specific socio-cultural problem. In the mid-70s, black radio stations in New York City, which had formerly acted as a cohesive oral glue for black communities — playing black music for black people — alienated their traditional audience by shifting to a playlist designed to attract more affluent — and white — demographics by mixing syrupy, de-funkified disco with slightly funkified white rock by the likes of Rod Stewart and The Rolling Stones. Fortunately for black communities, technology — in the form of audiomix tapes and portable stereos — filled the gap, supplying an alternative means of accessing music and sharing culture; namely *boom boxes*. The move to muzzle black radio also spurred the popularity of street parties in the Bronx, where the music that was no longer heard on the radio — funky black music by the likes of James Brown, Parliament Funkadelic, and Sly Stone, as well as mind-expanding tunes by Gil Scott-Heron and The Last Poets — could again be enjoyed and shared publicly. The fact that Kool Herc, the Jamaican MC, was on hand to power up the block-party revolution with his massive Jamaican-style sound system and his "toasting" or "shout-out" skills learned from legendary dub toasters like U Roy and Count Machouki, was fateful, adding oral fuel to the fire and helping set off a cultural revolution. And like both jazz and rock 'n' roll before it, this one has been demonized, exploited, regulated, targeted, pandered, and pimped ever since. And like its predecessors, rap and hip hop have not only endured, they have conquered the world.

Why do I call hip hop's four elements the four *oral* elements? Because the aims and principles of each of these artistic practices are unmistakably based on oral values. Let's start with the MC, the emcee, the rapper. Rappers are oral poets, exploiting language as sound, as experience, as self. Like all bards, rappers work with music and musicians. Rappers are performers and entertainers whose goal is to turn a crowd of individuals into a living community. The best rappers are fantastic improvisers — *freestylers* — extemporizing lyrics of extreme semantic and rhythmic complexity in fiery public competition. Rappers employ call-and-response. Rappers make liberal use of slang. Rappers blur distinctions between speech, chant, and song. Rappers celebrate non-semantic vocalizing (that is, beat-boxing). They are oralists.

The oral skills of Canibus, Eminem, and the late Biggie Smalls — to name but three revered freestylers — are astonishing. Their dense, high-speed, improvised riffing dances with lyrical invention, sophisticated rhythms, deft insights, and fluid mutations of tone, pace, and mood. Freestyle battles between MCs are the essence of the rapper's art and are akin to the "cutting sessions" that were once a mainstay of jazz. Just as jazz musicians tore into one another, determined to show whose chops were supreme, so do hip hopping MCs battle it out, dissing each other's talents, taste in clothes, and — of course — mamas. This dissing has long been familiar in black communities as "signifying" and "dozens," a pair of street-corner insult games whose aim was "to totally destroy someone else with words," as hip-hop chronicler Davey D puts it. But whereas "the dozens" and "signifying" are informal activities, freestyle battles are sometimes witnessed by thousands of fans, like the furious battle between East Coast king Biggie Smalls (a.k.a. Notorious B.I.G.) and West Coast hero Tupac Shakur before a raucous sold-out crowd at Madison Square Garden.

One of the most talented and brilliantly funny freestylers is the much-despised Eminem. Anyone who still thinks that this emotionally disturbed young freak lacks talent or brains need only listen to a few recordings of his many freestyle battles to recognize the scope of his satirical intelligence. But there are many, many other skilled freestylers out there, such as the entirely unknown Drop Dead Fred, from Cleveland. I once spent a few ear-opening hours under an old bridge with Fred. Few literate poets could imagine poetic virtuosity of the kind Fred is capable; hour after hour of verbal pyrotechnics and pointed social commentary spilling in exquisitely inventive rhymes and impeccably paced rhythms. Anytime. Anywhere. For as long as you can take it.

The connection between rapping and orality is fairly obvious. But graffiti art is a visual medium. How can it be an oral art form? Because, despite the fact that it is a form of writing, graffiti art sacrifices written language by stripping graf letters of literal meaning. It injects personality and context into textuality with a percussive stew of calligraphic idiosyncrasies, formal geometries, and exsanguinate illness. It embraces transience and decay. It celebrates individual creativity yet remains largely anonymous. On freights and subways and cube vans, it travels, subverting the literate insistence on art staying in its place, on the shelf, or in the museum. Graffiti art — both piecing and tagging — is a dialogue, a meta-tale recording an urban journey, a parade of icons asserting implied relationships through indirection, suggestion, glimpses of past presence in the passing present. Graf is a form of city-surfing, a virtual web of tingling, aerosol-sniffing freaks, a chorus of loud shout-outs, a community of crews engaged in kinetic poetics.

Most of which also applies to hip-hop dancing, which isn't just breakdancing but popping and locking and electric boogie too; it travels, it's performative, it's transient, it's public, it's playful, it's done in groups, it's done in freewheeling competition, it's antiphonal, it's open to all, it's improvised, it has no fourth wall. The development of technique consists almost exclusively of the idiosyncratic elaboration of a personal style. *It's all oral.*

Deejaying is part of the same oral matrix, but its significance extends far beyond that of hip-hop culture. Historically, hip-hop DJs are among the first postmodern folk artists. Unschooled ghetto kids instinctively treated turntables and LPs like Andy Warhol used images and media — as subject matter. They tossed out instruction manuals and refashioned technology in their own oral image, creating antiphonal dance music from bits and pieces of pop tunes. The origin of scratching lies in playing two copies of the same record on adjacent turntables and switching rapidly back and forth between them, playing the same funky drum breaks over and over again: let the record go, hit the mixer, and while the two-second beat plays, reset the second LP, let it go, hit the mixer, and reset the first LP. Again and again, rocking back and forth, creating a living, sweating mix and a fundamental subversion of the integrity of the musical artifact. Jamming, improvising, creating, responding to the audience. You like this beat? I'll play it again, and again and again. And now I'll start messing with it, scratching it back and forth like screaming sandpaper, chopping and dropping beats and laying tracks on top of each other in surreal collages: Afrika Bambaata of the Black Spades up in the Bronx back in 77, plugging into a street light for power and rocking the block with massive ear-splitting speakers; Malcolm X's inspired preaching resounding between project towers layered over Kraftwerk over Earth, Wind and Fire over Parliament Funkadelic's anthemic grooves.

And scratching — when DJs became producers and hit the studio — led to sampling. Instead of playing the same break over and over in real time, why not sample it — record it digitally — and play it back through a MIDI-controlled keyboard? Why use musicians when the entire catalogue of recorded sound is available as a musical palette? Cut and paste, mix and match, borrow and blend. This is before personal computers. This is before the World Wide Web. This is before digital culture. And yet it *is* digital culture. Sampling and deejaying are pure digitalisms. Hip-hop DJs and producers succeeded — in ways that literate theorists could only hint at — in unearthing the cut-and-paste ethos latent in digital technology. They didn't care about copyright, any more than graf bombers cared who owned the subways. They cared about creativity. Technology became a subordinate tool rather than a tyrant dictating the terms of engagement. Sound was just information.

This was a revolutionary concept, and it quickly caught the attention of the economic empire of literate culture. Its legalists soon recognized the dangerously disruptive potential these poor black kids represented. *Because hip-hoppers were behaving as if sound didn't belong to anybody except the people using it.* Which — for oralists — it doesn't. They didn't care about the legal, authorial, economic, or material sanctity of the oral archives that were their record collections. *They lived in sound*, and their values were based on the exploitation of the creative potential of sound.

So the literate economists tried to shut oral values down by regulating sampling. And it worked, to some degree. Experimentation and sampling *has* been slowed up since the record labels began suing kids for making highly original sound collages that include snippets of other people's music. (The legalized lifting of entire verses and grooves by the likes of Puffy Combs to create execrable formulaic rip-offs of sublime tunes by the Jackson 5 or Stevie Wonder is one result of the outlawing of freewheeling sampling and the sanctioning of expensive and bureaucratic "chorus" licensing.) And yet the damage had been done; the genie of black creative genius had busted loose again.

And to top it off, literate culture was about to do neo-oralists a huge favour. It was about to do itself in. The hyperliterate sphere of science had discovered the mathematical key to the Pythagorean universe and was about to unleash the extraordinary magic of digital technology on the world.

What was the first digitally driven challenge to the fundamental economic integrity of literate culture? Napster. With 73 million subscribers (before it was shut down in 2001) enthusiastically asserting that file sharing is the essential aim and purpose of digital technology and that the concept of copyright is meaningless in the digital realm — the cut-and-paste future became palpable. And who was the most outspoken and aggressive supporter of Napster? Which musician most consistently articulated the importance of Napster as a political tool? Who has been leading the charge on literate values? Chuck D — a black man, a rapper, a postliterate revolutionary.

Chuck D is hip-hop's greatest MC — bar none. Nobody else speaks with his combination of exceptional moral intelligence, creative ambition, and raw poetic power. Unlike many MCs with larger-than-life personas that are entirely invented, Chuck D has always striven to walk his talk. Along with his alter ego, that knowing fool, Flavor Flav, Chuck Ridenhour has been the frontman for Public Enemy since 1986 when the group recorded its first album, *Yo! Bum Rush the Show*. Public Enemy has since recorded album after album of hard-hitting poetry dealing with blackness, America, and a wide range of social issues. The group has always had a tempestuous relationship with the media — largely because they miss no opportunity to point out its endless hypocrisies. Flavor Flav even took on the print world directly in his song "Letter to the New York Post." (The *Post* had played up Flav's legal troubles, specifically his conviction for domestic assault.) Public Enemy's popularity has waned since the group had a huge hit with "Don't Believe the Hype" in 1989. Yet ironically the group's recordings just keep getting better and better.

But Chuck D isn't alone. He may be the apex, but many other powerful postliterates have pushed hip hop to sublime creative heights. His near-peers include Spearhead's Michael Franti — whose lone *Disposable Heroes of Hiphoprisy* CD is among the greatest poetic works of the 90s — along with Tupac Shakur, Guru, De la Soul, the Beastie Boys, Biggie Smalls, Outkast, and maybe Aceyalone of Freestyle Fellowship. But my biases are clearly old school. Someone else might choose to celebrate Common, Dilated Peoples, Xzibit, Wyclef Jean, Kool Keith, Eminem, DMX, Busta Rhymes, Mos Def, Dr. Dre, Method Man, or any number of other popular rappers. There is a lot of oral talent out there.

There are no women on my short list, not because Missy Elliot or L'il Kim or Queen Latifah or Salt-N-Pepa or Lauryn Hill or Bahamadia or

Michie Mee aren't all smart and talented. They are. And maybe one or all of them would be on your list of the greatest MCs. But although times have changed in black America, for women they aren't that different today from almost forty years ago when James Brown sang "It's a Man's Man's Man's Man's World." And it's not just that there aren't many female MCs or bombers or breakers. It's something deeper. And it has to do with the idea of the reconciliation of the word with the body.

In the introduction to *News of the Universe*, a collection of essays and poems about nature, Robert Bly argues that there is a deep connection between the way individuals and communities treat women, nature, and the unconscious. He suggests that, historically, when a society shows respect to one of these three it usually respects the others equally. By the same token, when one of them is degraded, the others often are as well. Bly's formulation appears particularly relevant to hip hop, where nature is utterly ignored and women are viciously disrespected.

I suggested in a previous chapter that black pop-music lyrics in the 60s and 70s were unable to fully channel the repressed anger and hurt felt by black Americans, that the lyrics failed to sink wells into certain tempestuous zones of the collective unconscious, that such wells were still to be dug. It's apparent now that hip hop is such a well. Not surprisingly, part of what has flowed from it is a tremendous amount of anger, both residual and current. Most of that anger is self-directed, however, like the black-on-black violence ripping American neighbourhoods apart. The anger has been unlocked, but it's not been overcome. And I'm not saying that black-on-white violence would be any kind of solution. What I'm saying is that — even though in hip hop we finally find the long-awaited return of the black word to black music — this reconciliation is missing something vital, something else must be reclaimed to successfully transmute the destructive legacy of repressed pain through poetry, something must facilitate the journey to the vulnerability necessary before healing can begin. And that something is respect for women's power, women's knowledge, and women's needs.

In hip hop, disrespect for women is rampant and often almost pathological. Despite the humility required for truly inventive freestyling, which is the unfettered articulation of unconscious ideas, images, and feelings, most rapping is extremely egotistical, positing a macho invulnerability that refuses a genuine examination of selfhood and its inevitable frustrations and insecurities. If male MCs were willing to sacrifice their supermen personas and instead acknowledge their vulnerability and their need for women's strength, hip hop could become (as a minority of "conscious" hip-hoppers have always tried to make it) a powerful tool for collective and individual healing.

But for that to happen, the national war on black men would have to stop. And that doesn't look likely as America enters the reign of George the Second. The prison-industrial complex has, in a few short years, grown in significance to the point where it is now the greatest scourge facing black Americans since the CIA invited Manuel Noriega to use American ghettos as retail markets for his cocaine. The statistics are mind-boggling: on any given day, one-third of black American men will be in jail, on parole, or on probation. In some states, black men are fifty times more likely to be imprisoned than white men convicted of identical drug offences. Blacks now make up nearly 60 per cent of all Americans admitted into prisons each year, despite numbering only 15 per cent of the American population. And these are privately owned prisons, that force prisoners to work for pennies while reselling their labour at a tremendous profit, thereby adding to the incentive to lock up greater numbers of quasi-criminals. Ten- and fifteen-year mandatory minimum sentences are all the rage for relatively harmless non-violent offences. Three strikes and you're in. For life.

As Black American youth were busy building a means of engaging the world on their terms, building a cultural movement that at last gave them a voice to articulate their material and spiritual reality in words, white America was busy pulling a fast one. Just as black America generated an ambitious and potent word-language, white America was recapturing and imprisoning the black body.

With that kind of evil hanging over black America, along with the urban blight, the poverty, the drugs, the broken homes, and the heavy baggage of its preceding generations, the transformative potential of its oral poetry is perhaps limited. And yet, if organized resistance to institutionalized discrimination is to come, it may be inspired by hip-hop MCs, by lyrical songs falling from the lips of a nation in crisis. Which is why, perhaps, the most charismatic and influential rapper of recent years, Tupac Shakur, son of a Black Panther, who captured the hearts and ears of millions of American youth, both black and white, men and women, was gunned down just as he was maturing from a gangbanging adolescent to a freethinking, outspoken, and media-savvy black man. He was turning into a leader. And like so many black American leaders, he died young, in a hail of gunfire and a pool of blood.

21 Flippin' the Script

At the dawn of the twenty-first century, with rock 'n' roll a half-century old, hip hop a quarter-century old, and the World Wide Web already ancient though still an infant, a survey of the cultural landscape reveals this startling phenomenon: there has been an extraordinary switcheroo. The fundamental dichotomy articulated in this book — black oral wordlessness versus white literate disembodiedness — has been reversed. A quick comparison of American youth cultures shows that predominantly black hip-hopping youth are intoxicated with words, and predominantly white techno-obsessed youth have abandoned words and embraced a musical movement based almost exclusively on the relationship of the body to sound.

Each youth culture is reacting to the changing dynamics of American communication paradigms that, for the past few decades, have been reevaluated and redefined as a result of the evolution of electronic technology and the gradual imposition of its hierarchy of values. Each group has been targeted — in different ways — by the media, which has unleashed upon it an onslaught of confusing and awesomely exploitative images, and each group has responded in its own way.

Most rap music has willingly submitted itself to the media-industrial complex, sacrificing its oral values in exchange for a wholesale commodification of its look, sound, and energy. The reconciliation of black words and music and the reclamation of an articulate and public black word-language has yielded little in the way of political empowerment for speakers or their listeners. Part of the reason for this situation, as mentioned, may be the exclusion of women's voices, identities, and knowledge from the rap dialogue and the prevailing machismo, which resists genuine self-examination. But of equal significance is that "the meaning of the words" is determined in part by the economy that shapes, packages, and sells them; by the hegemony that controls them and renders them safe, subservient, and impotent.

What aspiring young rappers fail to grasp as they wait eagerly to sign on the dotted major-label line — and what savvy veterans like KRS-1 and Chuck D keep trying to tell them — is they are getting played by buying into an industry that constantly and aggressively reinforces the infrastructure of racism. Signing a record deal with Warner Music means signing on as a cog in the vast media-entertainment-cable-internet conglomerate that is AOL Time Warner. It means participating in an industry that systematically ignores the widespread discrimination experienced by black Americans — by people of colour all over the world — in favour of focusing on the joys (and puerile tragedies) of being white and wealthy on TV shows like *Survivor*, *The West Wing*, *Ally McBeal*, *Beverly Hills 90210*, and *One Life to Live*. It means buying into an industry that attacks "gangsta" rappers for promoting a perverted immorality, while it makes millions selling their CDs to its (white) children, who have been mesmerized by music-video marketing into thinking that a few "playas" lip-syncing while surrounded by "bitches" in bikinis represents "authentic" culture and "real" emotion, something they desperately crave because the rest of the crap served up by the media is transparently irrelevant. It means submitting again to the demands of the literate mindset, which sees music — especially black music — as a dangerous force to be captured and caged before being bought and sold, rather than as an experience to be shared and valued on its own terms.

Ironically, rap has become a tool of the literate economy, and thus implicitly reinforces its values. It's happened before, of course, but this time the co-opt is far more subtle. Because although it *appears* that rap has successfully reclaimed an articulate word-language, because black men and women are standing proud and telling you what they think of you, of themselves, and of their world, their presence has been cleverly colonized by the literate empire. Not only are the social values of much rap profoundly materialistic and thus simplistically reinforce an economically oppressive social structure, but in formal terms the music industry has managed to refashion rap into a literate shadow of its original oral self.

Specifically, the media-entertainment complex has *elevated reproduction over improvisation in hip hop*. Despite the importance of freestyling and battling within the original b-boy culture, contemporary rap aesthetics are dictated by mass marketing of mass products rather than real-time encounters between real people. *It has hidden the creative process from public view*. Whereas early hip hop was geared toward the live event at which DJs created a live mix by playing with turntables, the creative focus — and locus — of today's rap industry is the recording studio. Rappers do gigs as afterthoughts, to support their albums, and they often deliver half-assed live performances of four or five songs. They're like writers forced in front of a lectern without a clue how to act. And it's true that soul and R & B and jazz and blues musicians also recorded in recording studios, hidden from the public eye. But Charles Mingus, John Lee Hooker, Dinah Washington, and Aretha Franklin could always *make it new* onstage. They saw the recording process as a means to an end, not as the primary medium of their creativity. They developed their style and skills as part of — and with an absolute commitment to — an oral culture that trained them in the art of moving a crowd. That ability was always the bedrock of their creative practice. Not so for today's rappers. They work in studios and basements, recording demos and dreaming of hit songs and expensive videos. They make music the same way writers write books. In isolation.

But the greatest subversion of hip hop's oral integrity and the music industry's most important imposition of literate values on it, is the fundamental redefinition of key aspects of hip hop as product rather than process. Instead of a creative experience that exists in real time, that welcomes dialogue and responds in the moment to external stimuli, that includes rather than excludes, that responds to community needs rather than industry needs, that challenges spectators to participate rather than challenges them to consume, corporate America has sought to make hip hop a closed shop; rewarding those who buy into the system with fame, while pocketing the serious cash and giving nothing back to communities.

Black recording artists in the 30s, 50s, and even 60s had little option but to submit to the demands of the music industry if they were to have a recording career. That is far from the case today. Not just because recording technology is cheap and omnipresent, but more important still, because the means of distribution are no longer concentrated in industry hands — which just makes the sell-out of black popular music to the old regime that much more disappointing. For the first time ever, there is a potential alternative to the sell-out, an alternative economic infrastructure and global marketplace that permits artists to engage directly with their fans without relying on the medium of the record label. The Internet has already demonstrated the potential to radically reshape human communication paradigms (think e-mail, Web sites, chat rooms), but digital culture is still being held in check by literate economic interests and values. As the digital generation matures, however, and begins to reshape the world in its own image, that will change.

The first and most substantial example of what digital values mean when large numbers of people embrace them on their own terms is rave culture. Rave culture implicitly and explicitly embraces digital values, as can be seen in its elevation of the DJ to pop-stardom status. For those who are not part of rave culture, who have not internalized postliterate values, the notion that the artistry of the DJ playing records is equal or superior to that of the people who made the records is absurd and demonstrably false. (And I don't even mean DJs with fancy behind-the-back scratching moves, although DJ contests can be extraordinarily creative postliterate events, combining improvisation with performance with technology with music in a fiery display of data manipulation). I mean the guys and girls who simply choose and play the records, *who create the live mix*. But to ravers and other techno-culturalists, it is the creation of the live mix, the manipulation of raw data, the recreation of reality in one's image that is the essence of the creative act. The product, like the source of the data, is irrelevant. It's all about process.

Hip hop first broke this ground in the popular consciousness, exploding the integrity and sanctity of the recorded artifact in pop music by inventing scratching and madcap mixing. And although the music industry — in part by regulating sampling — gradually reined in much of hip hop's experimentalism, the ground had been broken, the trail blazed in the popular consciousness. As the first quasi-digital generation began partying in the late 80s and early 90s, the creative vitality and innovative approach to sound that had characterized early hip hop began to find expression in a wide range of technology-based dance music styles. So it's not surprising that Afrika Bambaata, considered one of hip hop's greatest pioneers and producers, has gradually shifted his creative energy to Europe, because he has found there the same subversive intensity and musical adventurousness hip hop once possessed. Above all, he found that rave culture and its music — drum 'n' bass, jungle, house, deep house, acid jazz, electronica, trip-hop, trance, and many other musical styles — share many of hip hop's values, *his* values, the values that shaped his musical and cultural evolution: community, improvisation, the live event, experimentation, funk, play. Bambaata the ghetto oralist — by remaining true to himself and following his values — has become a global techno-freak.

Today's digitally-oriented youth have created a vast and vibrant musical culture that is nearly wordless. Although there are exceptions, especially songs that have garnered mainstream airplay by the likes of Chemical Brothers or Moby or Prodigy, most extended mixes feature only a smattering of words and rarely include anything that resembles traditional lyrics. Words are just one sound source, used for effect when needed, but of limited importance. The primary reason for this is that digital youth love to dance for hours, lost in an immersive artificial reality, blissed out on E, reeling in a delicious, delirious daze, a swirl of sweating bodies enveloped in sound, glued together by sound, entranced by sound and moving as one to its subtly shifting rhythms and timbres. In that context, extended lyrics are intrusive, anchoring the listener in time, place, reality. But dropped like bombs, slurred like honey, sliced and diced by samplers, they are welcome, adding depth to the moment without requiring conscious attention.

Today's youth have not entirely abandoned words, however, just music lyrics. Oral poetry is still valued, but its context is no longer musical: it is "spoken-word" culture. The spoken-word movement was initially dismissed by greying cultural critics as a retro phenomenon, as a harkening back to Beat culture, a revisiting of antique hipness. But the Beats were far less important catalysts of spoken word than were rappers, feminists, punk music, and the media itself. To the extent that spoken-word poets looked to an older generation of oral poets, they found inspiration in the work of rock 'n' roll heroes like Patti Smith, Jello Biafra, and Jim Morrison rather than in Ferlinghetti or Kerouac. It was the vitality and depth of youth culture — always and everywhere centred on music, especially rock and hip hop — that laid the foundation for the rise of spoken word.

But spoken word is not a product of music alone. It is the result of a confluence of forces that have affirmed the validity and heightened the social value of individual voices. These forces include the impact of electronic-communications technologies that impose a form of postliterate orality. Although distinct in essential ways from preliterate orality, this neo-orality reaffirms such traditional oral values as publicness, transience, personality, and the privileging of the voice itself. Another key force that helped trigger and nurture the spoken-word movement was feminism — not just because so many spoken-word poets are women, nor just because feminism opened the door to the popular telling of women's tales, but rather because feminism advocated and to a large extent succeeded in breaking down the bedrock of narrative authority. This shift from a literate narrative hegemony — *he who writes books writes history* — to postliterate narrative multiplicity — *she who speaks her story creates her history* — is one of the key dynamics of postmodernism. And yet these forces (feminism, television, rock'n'roll) were in play in 1975 and in 1985. Why was it only in the early 90s that the spoken-word movement took off? The answer is that once again poetry took its cue from black music, and in this case the catalyst was hip hop.

As hip-hop culture gained popularity among American youth, rap attuned the popular ear to poetic language divorced from its traditional performative dependence on melody. Rap's exceptional poetic potency — along with its nearness to natural speech — had a profound impact on non–hip hoppers. Confronted by rappers their own age exuberantly working the mic, both white and black middle-class youth who had been socialized into a predominantly literate world yet who possessed a profound quasi-latent allegiance to oral values were inspired to tell their stories. And as rap grew in popularity and deepened in scope, North American adolescents and young adults were made more aware of the inadequacy of print as a tool with which to fulfill their expressive needs or articulate their identities. The result was a sense of "Hey, I can do that." Or, for the many performance poets unable or unwilling to embrace the MC paradigm, "Hey, I can do *my version* of that. I can tell *my story*. I can make up my own poems. And I don't need a band. I'll just *speak*."

Unfortunately, however, in its collective immaturity spoken-word culture often ranks poets by the scars they claim to bear. All too often the standard applied by audiences and peers alike in determining the quality of spoken-word poems is the poet's purported identity, rather than the quality of the performative energy and language shaping the poetic event. Moreover, because spoken word is a youth-driven culture, its practitioners typically display little understanding of the vast and rich heritage of oral poetic practices from which they might learn and grow. As a result, the tone and form of spoken-word poems tend to be monotonous and derivative. However, spoken-word culture still offers youth a valuable arena in which to learn, share, and explore collective and individual imaginations. Occasionally, it also produces some stunning poetry.

Ultimately, however, the key obstacle to the maturation of spoken-word culture into a socially, culturally, and economically significant poetic movement is — still and again — the hegemony of the text. With rare exceptions, spoken-word poets have failed to show the courage to break with the literate paradigm and commit fully to the oral. As a result, their efforts are half-baked. They will not, for example, sacrifice the safety of the fourth wall; they have not adopted a polyphonic or antiphonal model but rather that of serial monologues; they do not dance, and often seem to wish that their bodies would just go away; they often read from written texts; they don't improvise. Their work is barely oral. It is literacy masquerading as orality.

One group of contemporary poets that has been influenced by spoken-word culture and U.K. dub poetry, and possesses truly oral values, is comprised of the drum 'n' bass and junglist MCs; folks like MC L Natural and Caddy Cad. These MCs *do* dance, they *do* improvise, they *do* antiphony, they *do* technology. They aren't rappers, they're riffers. Moreover, in keeping with the neo-hippie aesthetic of the rave culture umbrella, these poets unhesitatingly reference the cosmic dimension. They willingly launch themselves into imaginative flight without fear of failure or concern for where their riffs might lead. It'll be a long, long party. No need to get too caught up in this or that line or metaphor. Just move. That's it. Dance. Dance. Dance. It's just poetry.

In rave culture, the postliterate neo-oral mindset has been allowed to bloom. Why postliterate and neo-oral? Because unlike literate culture, *rave culture values context*; raves take place away from everyday life in isolated spaces that integrate designed elements into the existing natural environment to create a unique and organic whole. *It values community*; the tribalism of rave culture is explicitly celebrated in — among other things — its slogan, PLUR (Peace, Love, Unity, Respect). *It values elasticity of time, space, body, and self*; rave culture consistently seeks to blur fixed borders established by literate culture, celebrating Ecstasy (the drug) as a tool and ecstasy (the state) as a legitimate spiritual goal. *It emphasizes process*; the creative energy of techno music is out in the open at raves, with kids hauling their samplers, sequencers, drum machines, computers, and p.a. systems out into open fields and creating digital music in public.

What this means is that ironically — or perhaps tragically — it appears that hip hop is doing a disservice to black culture by integrating black music ever more effectively into a literate economy that is not only explicitly exploitative of black creativity, but is itself in the process of being eclipsed by the digital economy. It means that black America has reclaimed its apparently potent public language in a socio-economic context that renders it increasingly irrelevant.

As Napster — to cite one example — made clear, literacy's previously inexorable colonization of oral space has been forced into a defensive, reactive mode by the ascendance of hyper-efficient digital communication technologies. Oralists have much to gain from the digital future, which has much more in common with oral than with literate values. For example, digital culture renders time fluid. And although the fluidity of digital time is fundamentally different from the fluidity of oral time (the former is based on the absolute presence of communication and the latter on its absolute evanescence), they are nonetheless far more similar to each other than either is to the fixed and managed chronology of literate life, in which every second is noted and measured, bought and sold.

In this context, it's also worth considering the legal concept of copyright, which ultimately undid Napster. The word itself expresses its function and origin in a convenient though unintended pun: copyright fixes the rights associated with the copying of writing. Copyright did not exist as a concept until print made the copying of writing possible on a mass scale in the sixteenth century and thereby laid the foundation for both the publishing industry and intellectual property law. Before this, there had been little reason to question who owned an idea or poem as there existed neither the means to easily copy and distribute it nor — in a largely oral world — a method to determine its origin. Print technology permitted copying on an unprecedented scale and also allowed for authorship to be traced, thus giving birth to the notion of copyright. The point is that copyright is an arbitrary concept that arose as a logical —and inevitable — response to the development of a revolutionary new communication technology: the printing press. As Marshall McLuhan was among the first to point out, we are experiencing another such revolution as electronic digital technology gains ascendance. Napster's utter disregard for that most cherished of literate principles, intellectual property, is the logical — the inevitable — popular response to the development of a revolutionary new communications technology: the Internet. From a digital perspective, copyright is a quaint and somewhat primitive notion mattering no more to digital economics than gift-giving mattered to literate capitalists.

Nobody today can predict what a fully developed digital economy will look like other than to say it will bear little resemblance to the literate economy dominating our society at present. I am convinced that digital culture will ultimately come to value process far more than product. Digital technology makes digital products economically redundant because they can be infinitely reproduced at virtually no cost and also because authorship is irrelevant in cut-and-paste culture, making a product-based economy of ideas difficult to maintain in the long run. Thus what comes to have value is not the thing but the making of the thing — like the DJ doing live mixes, manipulating data, engaged in digital wizardry — privileging oralists who are skilled in collaborative process and collective creativity.

Whereas literacy and orality historically have been antagonists, digital culture may offer a dialectical synthesis of these two old foes. Literacy is not being abandoned as a tool. People want and need to read, just as they wanted and needed to continue speaking after learning to write. Digital culture is itself impossible without eyes that can decipher complex visual codes. Software is *written*. The key difference is that while print culture was able to impose its values on the technology of speech and thereby shape both individual and collective psychologies, the technology of binary code is now about to impose digital values upon the world as it gradually usurps literate dominance.

This development brings us to the digital divide, and the point at which this fluid tale takes on a hard, material meaning. In America today, in the world today, people of colour are largely absent from the Internet, excluded from participation in the digital revolution. Participation requires money; money for computers but also for education, for network infrastructure, for electrical power infrastructure. Huge swaths of the of-colour world are missing these things, and so are unable to engage with the digital future. Having barely been able to come to terms with the exigencies of literate economics, having, in fact, been maintained in a state of dependency by means of literate tools, the threat of an equally unjust digitally enabled future looms. As the clock ticks in the twenty-first century and the digital economy begins to process and distribute a greater percentage of the world's dollars, the state of enforced wordlessness that characterized African slaves when they were brought to America is being replicated. Whites are using their mastery of literacy to stake out a massive edge in the digital realm, inventing tools with which to — again — reshape the world in their image. And again they are excluding peoples of colour, again setting the terms, again creating a communication paradigm that will enrich the few — of whom the vast majority will be white — at the expense of the many — of whom the vast majority will not. We've come full circle. The digital divide is a form of renewed enslavement.

Is there any hope that this process can be reversed, redirected, reclaimed? Absolutely. First, it is early. The war of digital values on literate values hasn't even begun in a serious way yet. The technology is still immature. In 2010, when 60 to 70 per cent of North American households will likely have broadband access to the Internet, the neo-oralists may be in a position to make a far greater impact than they have to date. Perhaps then the black creative genius that took esoteric novelty technologies like the saxophone and electric guitar and remade them into global icons of extraordinary significance, that elevated the turntable from functional tool to musical instrument, may yet work its magic on the utilitarian Internet.

For that to happen, the digital divide will need to be bridged. That doesn't simply mean getting more computers into classrooms, though that's a start. What is needed is for progressive oralists, literates, and digitalists to work together so that strategic advances can be designed and implemented to push forward empowerment on all three fronts. It's what hip-hop activists Davey D and Chuck D have been doing with sites such as attackradio.com, rapstation.com, and Davey D's e-mail newsletter, *Friday Nite Vibe*. Davey D, for example, hooked up his tens of thousands of weekly readers with the Black Radical Congress's instructive and incisive articles, delivered by e-mail to desktops around the world on a daily basis. That's the kind of simple yet powerful digital activism (I call it *interactivism*) that can make a difference. And, of course, speaking as a white guy, those of us who are positioned to help bridge the digital divide from a place of power must do so. Because if one of us ain't free, then none of us is free. And that's not just a slogan.

So where will the momentum lie? Will the bigots and narrow-minded, greedy, fearful folks — of whatever colour — be on the inside or on the outside? Will you be singing the Digitopia Blues? Or will you be saying, "Goddam. We levelled this playing field."? That's the question and the challenge. Oral poets have a role to play here. The digital realm is made for them. Although exactly what postliterate poetry will look like, I can't say yet. But I'm headed that way. And looking out for fellow travellers.

Notes

1. Danny Barker, recorded interview with author, July 1989.
2. Francis Bebey, *African Music: A People's Art* (London: Harrap, 1975), 115.
3. Bebey, 115.
4. Ben Sidran, *Black Talk: How the Music of Black America Created a Radical Alternative to the Values of Western Literary Tradition* (New York: Da Capo, 1986), 6.
5. Malcolm X, *Malcolm X Speaks: Selected Speeches and Statements*, ed. George Breitman (New York: Merit Publishers, 1965).
6. "Rivers of Babylon," B. Dowe/F. MacNaughton, Ackee Music, 1972.
7. Julio Finn, *The Bluesman* (London, Quartet Books, 1986), 109.
8. Ralph Ellison, *Shadow and Act* (New York: Vintage, 1995), 242.
9. Brian Priestly, *Mingus: A Critical Biography* (Da Capo: New York, 1984), 114.
10. Billy Taylor, "Negroes Don't Know Anything About Jazz" in *The Jazz Word*, ed. Dom Cerulli, Burt Korall, Mort L. Nasatir (New York: Da Capo, 1987), 40.
11. Mezz Mezzrow, *Really the Blues* (New York: Citadel Press, 1990), 53–54.
12. Tin Pan Alley is the generic name given to the songwriting and sheet-music publishing industry that flourished in America between 1890 and 1950.
13. Neil Leonard, *Jazz: Myth and Religion* (New York: Oxford, 1987), 108.
14. "A Fine Romance," lyrics by Dorothy Fields © Universal Music Publishing.

15. "Strange Fruit," lyrics by Lewis Allen, © Music Sales Corp.
16. Billie Holiday, *Lady Sings the Blues* (New York: Penguin, 1986), 84.
17. "God Bless the Child," by Billie Holiday, © Edward B Marks Music Company.
18. "Lush Life," lyrics by Billy Strayhorn, © Music Sales Corp.
19. Ezra Pound, *ABC of Reading* (New York: New Directions, 1960), 206.
20. "Heebie Jeebies," scatting by Louis Armstrong, song by Boyd Atkins, © Universal Music Publishing.
21. Danny Barker, recorded interview with author, July 1989.
22. Danny Barker, recorded interview with author, July 1989.
23. "It's the Tune That Counts," by Jan Savitt and Don Raye, © Universal Music Publishing.
24. Slim Gaillard, *Jazz Voices,* ed. Kitty Grime (London: Quartet Books, 1983), 111.
25. Jerome Rothenberg, ed., *Technicians of the Sacred: A Range of Poetries from Africa, America, Asia, Europe and Oceania* (Berkeley: University of California Press, 1985), 442.
26. Stanley Dance, *The World of Duke Ellington* (New York: Da Capo, 1970), 7.
27. Neil Leonard, *Jazz: Myth and Religion* (New York: Oxford, 1987), 108.
28. Mezzrow, 222.
29. Mezzrow, 223.
30. "A Love Supreme," poem published by MCA records on sleeve of album, *A Love Supreme.*
31. J. C. Thomas, *Chasin' the Trane* (New York: Da Capo, 1975), 186–87.
32. "Driva Man," lyrics by Oscar Brown Jr., © Melma Publishing Company.
33. Max Roach, liner notes to *We Insist! Freedom Now Suite* (New York: Candid Records, 1960).
34. Wallace Stevens, in *The Jazz Poetry Anthology*, ed. Sascha Feinstein and Yusef Komunyakaa (Bloomington: Indiana University Press, 1991–96), Vol. 1, 206.
35. Walt Whitman, "Song of Myself" (East Aurora: Roycroft, 1904), 1.
36. Vachel Lindsay, *Collected Poems* (MacMillan, New York, 1939), 23.
37. Vachel Lindsay, 23.
38. Vachel Lindsay, 23.
39. Carl Sandburg, *The Complete Poems of Carl Sandburg* (New York: Harcourt Brace Jovanovich, 1970), 179.
40. Carl Sandburg, *The American Songbag* (New York: Harcourt Brace Jovanovich, 1955), 250.
41. *The American Songbag*, 248.
42. *The American Songbag*, 238.
43. *The American Songbag*, 239.
44. *The American Songbag*, 236.

45. *The American Songbag*, 228.
46. Carl Sandburg, *100 American Poems*, ed. Selden Rodman (New York: Penguin Signet Books, 1948), 105.
47. MacLeish, Archibald, *A Time to Speak: The Selected Prose of Archibald MacLeish* (Boston: Houghton Mifflin, 1941), 68.
48. MacLeish, 90–91.
49. *The Collected Poems of William Carlos Williams*, ed. A. Walton Litz and Christopher MacGowan (New York: New Directions, 1986), Vol. 2, 1939–62, 394.
50. Stephen Cushman, *William Carlos Williams and the Meaning of Measure* (New Haven: Yale University Press, 1985), 1.
51. William Carlos Williams, *Yes, Mrs. Williams: A Personal History of My Mother* (New York: New Directions, 1982), 30.
52. Kerry Driscoll, *William Carlos Williams and the Maternal Muse* (Ann Arbor: UMI Research Press, 1987), 139–40.
53. *The Collected Poems of William Carlos Williams*, ed. A. Walton Litz and Christopher MacGowan (New York: New Directions, 1986), Vol. 1, 1909–39, 74.
54. Jack Kerouac, *The Jack Kerouac Collection* © Rhino Records, 1990.
55. Bruce Cook, *The Beat Generation* (New York: Scribner, 1971), 88.
56. Allen Ginsberg, *Composed on the Tongue* (Bolinas: Grey Fox Press, 1980), 43.
57. Lawrence Ferlinghetti, liner notes, *Poetry Readings at the Cellar* (Fantasy 1958).
58. Kenneth Rexroth, liner notes, *Poetry Readings at the Cellar* (Fantasy 1958).
59. Bob Dylan, *The Times They Are A-Changin'*, © M.Witmark and Sons.
60. Grace Slick, *Somebody to Love?* (Warner, New York, 1998), 7.
61. Cordell Reagon, *Everybody Says Freedom: A History of the Civil Rights Movement in Songs and Pictures*, ed. Pete Seeger and Bob Reiser (New York: Norton, 1989), 85.
62. Sam Block, in *Everybody Says Freedom*, 179.
63. Bruce Hartford, in *Everybody Says Freedom*, 207.
64. Bernice Johnson Reagon, in *Everybody Says Freedom*, 77.
65. Bernice Johnson Reagon, in *Everybody Says Freedom*, 77.
66. Brian Ward, *Just My Soul Responding: Rhythm and Blues, Black Consciousness and Race Relations* (Berkeley: University of California Press, 1998), 290.
67. Ellison, 255–57.
68. Curtis Mayfield, *Choice of Colors*, © 1969 Warner Tamerlane Publishing.
69. Larry Neal, "Afterword," in ed. Larry Neal and LeRoi Jones, *Black Fire: An Anthology of African American Writing* (New York: Morrow, 1968), 654–55.

70. Imamu Amiri Baraka, *The Music* (New York: Morrow, 1987), 244.
71. Stephen E. Henderson, *Understanding the New Black Poetry* (New York: Morrow, 1972), 30–31.
72. Ishmael Reed. "Neo-Hoo Doo Manifesto," in ed. Jerome Rothenberg and Pierre Joris, *Poems for the Millennium, Volume Two* (Los Angeles: University of California Press, 1998), 440–41.
73. Gil Scott-Heron, *Message to the Messenger*, © 1994 brouhaha music.

Index

Aceyalone, 123
acid jazz, 131
Africa, oral traditions and values, 6–9
African music, 7–8
African-Americans, 4–5, 124–26
  exclusion from digital culture, 135–37
  freedom of expression through jazz, 22–23
  oral identity of, 9–13
African-Americans. *See also* black literature; black poets; black writers; slavery
"All Africa," 57
"All of Me," 29
"All Shook Up," 88
Allen, Lewis, 30
Allen, Red, 107, 109
"America Eats Its Young," 98
American Songbag, The (anthology), 66–68
AOL Time Warner, 128
Armstrong, Louis, 3, 48, 85
  jazz conversations and, 21
  rhythm of, 117
  scat singing and, 28, 36–37, 41
art music, 84–85, 86
Asante, Molefi Kete, 82
"Autobiography," 83
Ayler, Albert, 94

Bahamadia, 123
Baker, Chet, 21
Baker, Laverne, 87
"Ball of Confusion," 97
Bambaata, Afrika, 117, 121, 131
Baraka, Amiri, 102, 109–10, 112–13
Barefield, Eddie, 39
Barker, Danny, 3–5
  on scat singing, 37–39
Barker, Blue Lou, 3, 4
Basie, Count, 15, 85
"Beans and Cornbread," 87
Beastie Boys, The, 123

Beatles, The, 89
Bebey, Francis, 7–8, 78
bebop, 84–85, 86–87
Bechet, Sidney, 17, 37
Belle Stars, The, 3–4
Berrigan, "Bunny," 48
Berry, Chu, 42
Bey, Hakim, 96
Biafra, Jello, 132
big bands, 21, 28–29, 85
Big Easy, The (movie), 4
Big Maybelle, 87
Biggie Smalls, 118, 120, 123
Bin Hassan, Umar, 112
Black Arts Repertory Theater/School, 110
"Black Dada Nihilismus," 109
black literature, 102–6
  Mumbo Jumbo, 103–5
Black Mass, A (play), 109–10
black poets, poetry and jazz collaborations, 107–13
Black Radical Congress, 137
Black Spades, 121
Black Talk (book), 8–9
black writers, 102–6
Blackwell, Otis, 88
Blakey, Art, 118
Block, Sam, 93
Blow, Kurtis, 117, 118
Blue Devil Orchestra, 15–16
blues, 14–16
  jazz and, 17, 25
  jump, 85, 87
  lyrics of, 15, 25–28, 89–90
  poetry of, 25
  voice of, 15
Bluesman, The (book), 12
Bly, Robert, 124
Bolden, Buddy, 17, 37
"Bottle, The," 110
Brown, James, 91, 95, 98, 119, 124
Brown, Lawrence "Butter," 21
Brown, Oscar Jr., 35
  Freedom Now Suite, 55–57
Brown, Ruth, 87
Burnshaw, Stanley, 69
Busta Rhymes, 123

Caddy Cad, 133
"Caledonia," 87
call-and-response technique, 21
Calloway, Cab, 3, 85
  jive and, 49
  scat singing and, 28, 38–40
Canibus, 120
Carmichael, Hoagy, 77–79
Cheatham, Doc, 39
Chemical Brothers, 131
"Chicago" (poem), 66
"Chocko Ma Fendo Hey," 4–5
"Choice of Colors," 98
Chuck D, 123, 128, 137
civil rights movement, black music and poetry in, 92–101
Clark, Kenny "Kook," 48, 118
Clinton, George, 97–98
Cocteau, Jean, 71–72
Cole, Richie, 43
Coleman, Ornette, 85
  free jazz and, 22, 94
Coltrane, John, 19, 85
  Bobby Timmons on, 53–54
  A Love Supreme, 51–54
Combs, Sean, 122
Comets, The, 88
Common, 123
Congo, The (A Study of the Negro Race) (poem), 64
copyright, 122, 123, 134–35
"Coreen Died on a Battlefield," 4
Cortez, Jayne, 112–13
Cosby, Bill, 100

Cotton Club, The (Cincinnati), 42
Crane, Hart, 68, 69
Crawford, James "Jockamo," 4
Crosby, Bing, 28
Crudup, Arthur, 88
cummings, e.e., 68, 69
Cushman, Stephen, 74–75

Daddy-O, 50
Dae, Sunny, 88
Daltrey, Roger, 97
Dan Parrish Orchestra, 71–72
dance, dancing
- to bebop, 87
- to digital music, 131
- to hip hop, 121
- to jazz of 1920s, 88–89
- to rock 'n' roll, 88
- *See also* Whitman, Walt

Davey D, 120, 137
Davidman, Joy, 69
Davis, Art, 51
Davis, Miles, 21, 87
De la Soul, 123
deejaying, 121–22
deep house, 131
Delaney, Joe, 8
Delaney, Paddy, 8
Dennis, Kenny, 108
Depression, The, 89
Dickenson, Vic, 107
Dilated Peoples, 123
disc jockeys, jiving commentaries of, 50
"Disposable Heroes of Hiphoprisy" (CD), 123
Dixie Cups, The, 4
Dixieland Jazz Band. *See* Original Dixieland Jazz Band
DMX, 123
Dolphy, Eric, 22, 94
"Don't Be Cruel," 88
"Don't Believe the Hype," 123
"Don't Call Me Nigger, Whitey, There's a Riot Going On," 97
"Don't Explain," 31
Downbeat Magazine, 42
"Downhearted Blues," 17, 25
Dr. Dre, 123
Dr. John, 3
Driscoll, Kerry, 76–77
"Driva' Man," 55–56
Drop Dead Fred, 120
drum 'n' bass, 131
Du Bois, W.E.B., 11
Dutchman, The (play), 110
Dylan, Bob, 89–90, 92, 111

Earth, Wind and Fire, 121
"East St. Louis Toodle-oo," 46
Edison, Sweets, 77
Eldridge, Roy, 21
electronica, 131
Ellington, Duke, 85, 118
- big band and, 21, 28
- Billy Strayhorn and, 32, 35
- jazz conversations and, 21
- on representation of reality in music, 46

Ellison, Ralph, 15–16, 96
Eminem, 120, 123
ESP records, 109
Europe
- 19th century assessment of Africa, 6
- oral poetry in, 62–63

Evans, Bill, 21
Evans, Gil, 21
Everybody Says Freedom: A History of the Civil Rights Movement in Songs and Pictures (book), 92–93

Everyman Dictionary of Music, 7

Ferlinghetti, Lawrence, 82–83, 132
"Fever," 88
Fields, Dorothy, 28–29
"Fine Romance, A," 28–29, 34
Finn, Julio, 12
Flavor Flav, 123
Fletcher Henderson Orchestra, 55
Franklin, Aretha, 91, 97, 129
Franti, Michael, 123
free jazz, 22, 94
"Freedom Day," 57
Freedom Now Suite (album), 55–57
Freelance Pallbearers, The (book), 103
Freestyle Fellowship, 123
Friday Nite Vibe (e-mail newsletter), 137
"Fuck Tha Police," 119

Gaillard, Slim, 41
Garrison, Jimmy, 51
Gaye, Marvin, 91, 98–99
"Georgia on My Mind," 29, 77
Gillespie, John Birks "Dizzy," 43, 48, 81, 87
  jazz conversations and, 21
Ginsberg, Allen, 69, 81–82
"God Bless the Child," 30–31
Gordy, Berry, 90, 99
gospel music, 11–12, 94–95
graffiti art, 120–121
Grandmaster Caz, 117
Grandmaster Flash, 117
Graves, Milford, 109
"Great Balls of Fire," 88
Greer, Sonny, 21, 85
Griffin, Johnny, 43
Guru, 123
Guthrie, Woody, 90

Hadi, Shafi, 108
Haley, Bill, 88
Hampton, Lionel, 80–81
Hartford, Bruce, 93
Hawkins, Barbara, 4
Hawkins, Coleman, 55–56
"Heebie Jeebies," 36–37
"Hellhound on My Trail," 15
Hemphill, Julius, 21
Henderson, Fletcher, 28, 85
Henderson, Stephen E., 102
Hendrix, Jimi, 98
Hill, Lauryn, 123
Hinton, Milt, 107
hip hop
  dancing, 121
  Gil Scott-Heron and, 111
  oral elements of, 117–26
  See also rap
Hodges, Johnny, 21
Holiday, Billie
  jazz conversations and, 21
  lyrics of songs recorded by, 26–27, 29–31
  scat singing and, 38
hoodoo songs, 12
Hooker, John Lee, 129
Hot Fives, 17
Hot Sevens, 17
house, 131
Hughes, Langston, 107–9

"I Cover the Waterfront," 42
Ice-T, 118
"Iko Iko," 3–5
"I'm in the Mood for Love," 42
improvisation
  in hip hop, 129
  in jazz, 21–22, 47
  in scat singing, 36–37
Impulse Records, 51

indie record labels, 91, 95
Innervisions (album), 99
Internet, 135, 136–37. *See also* technology
intonation contouring, 20
"Is You Is or Is You Ain't My Baby," 87
"It's All Right," 88
"It's the Tune That Counts," 41

Jackson 5, 122
Jackson, Brian, 110
Jagger, Mick, 91
James, Etta, 87
jazz
  African-American slang and, 45–50
  bebop, 84–85
  blues and, 17, 25, 26
  as conversation, 20–22
  free jazz, 22, 94
  Jack Kerouac and, 80–81
  A Love Supreme, 51–58
  "Lush Life," 32–35
  lyrics of, 26–28
  modern jazz, 84–85
  nicknames, 48
  origin of word, 47–48
  poetry collaborations and, 71–72, 82–84, 107–13
  recording technology and, 17
  rhythm in, 19–20, 117–18
  scat singing, 28, 36–41
  seductive nature of, 47–48
  as sound, 19–20
  as story, 22–23
  swing, 19–20, 28–29
  Tin Pan Alley and, 26
  William Carlos Williams and, 73–77
  See also improvisation; R & B
Jazz Canto Vol. I (album), 77
Jean, Wyclef, 123
Jefferson Airplane, 91
Jefferson, Eddie, 42–44
jive, 49–50
Jives of Dr. Hepcat, The, 49
Jivin with Jax (radio show), 50
"Johannesburg," 110
Johnson, James Weldon, 36, 104
Johnson, Osie, 107
Johnson, Robert, 15
Jones, Elvin, 51
Jordan, Louis, 87
jump blues, 85, 87
jungle, 131
"Just Friends," 29
Just My Soul Responding: Rhythm and Blues, Black Consciousness and Race Relations (book), 95

Keppard, Freddy, 37
Kern, Jerome, 28
Kerouac, Jack, 80–82, 132
King Pleasure, 42–43
Knepper, Jimmy, 108
Kool Herc, 50, 119
Kool Keith, 123
Kool Moe Dee, 118
Kraftwerk, 121
KRS-1, 117–18, 128
Kupferberg, Tuli, 91

Lady Sings the Blues (autobiography), 30
Lambert, Hendricks and Ross, 43
LaFaro, Scott, 21
Lake, Oliver, 21
Last Poets, The, 111–13, 119
"Lazy River," 77
Leiber, Jerry, 4

Lennon, John, 91
Leonard, Neil, 26–27
  on metaphor in jazz, 47
Letter from Home (album), 43, 44
"Letter to the New York Post," 123
Lewis, Jerry Lee, 88
L'il Kim, 123
Lincoln, Abbey, *Freedom Now Suite,* 56–57
Lindsay, Vachel, 64–65
literate vs. oral values, 6, 9, 105–6, 122–23, 127
Little Richard, 89
live mix, 130
LL Cool J, 118
love songs, of swing era, 28–29
Love Supreme, A (album), 51–54, 55, 58
"Lush Life," 32–35
lyrics
  of the blues, 15, 25–28, 90
  of civil rights songs, 94, 97
  in digital music, 131–32
  of Eddie Jefferson, 43–44
  of *Freedom Now Suite,* 56
  of "Lush Life," 34–35
  of "race records," 25
  of rock 'n' roll, 89–90, 91
  of scat music, 36–37, 39, 40, 41
  of songs recorded by Bessie Smith, 26–27
  of songs recorded by Billie Holiday, 26–27, 29–31

Machouki, Count, 119
MacLeish, Archibald, 69–70
Malcolm X, 8–9, 87, 121
Marsalis, Wynton, 3
Mayfield, Curtis, 98
MC L Natural, 133
McCartney, Paul, 91
McGrath, Thomas, 69
McGuinn, Roger, 91
Mel, Melle, 117, 118
Melodians, The, 9
"Message to the Messengers," 111
Method Man, 123
Mezzrow, Milton "Mezz," 90
  Bessie Smith's influence on, 25–26
  on jazz slang, 48–49
  on jive, 49
Michie Mee, 124
Millay, Edna, 68
Millinder, "Lucky," 48
Mingus, Charles, 22, 108, 109, 129
"Mississippi Goddam," 97
Missy Elliot, 123
Moby, 131
modern jazz, 84–85
Monk, Thelonius, 81, 87, 118
Monroe, Harriet, 66
Moody, James, 42, 43
"Moody's Mood," 42
Moonglows, The, 89
Morrison, Jim, 91, 132
Morrison, Van, 91
Morton, Jelly Roll, 17
Mos Def, 123
Moten, Bennie, 15
Mr. Hepster's (Not Webster's) Jive Dictionary, 49
Mulligan, Gerry, 21
Mumbo Jumbo (book), 103–4
"Muse-Sick-and-Hour-Mess-Age" (CD), 112
music industry
  in digital culture, 130
  influence on black music, 26–28, 95
  racism in, 95, 128
"My Generation," 97
"My Indian Red," 4

Nance, Roy, 21
Nanton, Joe "Tricky Sam," 21, 46
Napster, 122–123, 134–35
Native American songs, and black music, 4–5
Neal, Larry, 102, 105
"Neo-HooDoo Manifesto," 103
Neville Brothers, 5
New York Art Quartet, 109
News of the Universe (essays and poems), 124
Nichols, Herbie, 118
"Niggers Are Scared of Revolution," 112
"Night in Tunisia, A," 43
Nuruddin, Jalal, 112
NWA, 118–19

Olatunji, Babatunde, 57
"Old Man Blues," 46
Oliver, King, 117
Opera, 71
oral poetry, 61–70
oral vs. literate values, 6, 9, 105, 122–23, 127
orality, 6–9
orchestras
- Blue Devil Orchestra, 15–16
- Dan Parrish Orchestra, 71–72
- Paul Whiteman Orchestra, 28
- Sun Ra's Arkestra, 109–10

Original Dixieland Jazz Band, 17
Outkast, 123
"Over My Head I See Freedom in the Air," 93

Page, "Hot Lips," 48, 85
Parker, Charlie "Bird," 80, 81, 87
Parker, Maceo, 20
"Parker's Mood," 42
Parlan, Horace, 108
Parliament Funkadelic, 119, 121
Parrish, Dan, 71
Patchen, Kenneth, 69
Paul Whiteman Orchestra, 28
Pavageau, "Slow Drag," 48
Payne, Bennie, 39
Pena, Ralph, 77
Pepper, Art, 77
Pickett, Wilson, 91
Pieces of a Man (album), 110
poetry
- of blues, 25
- in civil rights songs, 92–101
- in Europe, 62–63
- of Hoagy Carmichael, 77–79
- and jazz collaborations, 71–72, 82–84, 107–13
- in lyrics of "Lush Life," 34–35
- oral, 61–70
- of William Carlos Williams, 73–77

Poetry (magazine), 66
Poetry Readings at the Cellar (album), 82–83
pop music, 84–85, 95–96
Porter, Lewis, 52
Pound, Ezra, 15, 34
Powell, Bud, 118
praise songs, *A Love Supreme*, 51–58
Presley, Elvis, 88
Priestly, Brian, 22
Prodigy, 131
Pryor, Richard, 100
Public Enemy, 112, 123
"Public Speech and Private Speech in Poetry" (article), 69
Puffy, 122

Queen Latifa, 123

R & B, 58, 85, 87, 95
    civil rights movement and, 96–97
radios, 89
Rain Man (movie), 4
Rainey, Ma, 25
Rakim, 118
rap, 50, 117–26, 127–29
rap artists, nicknames of, 48
rave culture, 131, 134
RCA, 39
Reagon, Bernice Johnson, 93, 94
Reagon, Cordell, 93
Really the Blues (book), 25–26
recording technology, jazz and, 17
Redding, Otis, 91, 97
Reed, Ishmael, 103–6
Reed, Lou, 91
Reiser, Bob, 92
"Respect," 97
"Respect Yourself," 97
"Return to Sender," 88
"Revolution Will Not Be Televised, The," 110
Rexroth, Kenneth, 83
rhythm
    in jazz, 19–20, 117–18
    in scat singing, 38
    variable foot of William Carlos Williams, 74–75
Ridenhour, Chuck, 123
riffers, 133–34
Roach, Max, 118
    Freedom Now Suite, 55–57
Robinson, Smokey, 91, 99
"Rock Around the Clock," 88
rock 'n' roll, 84–90
    lyrics of, 89–90, 91
Rolling Stones, The, 119
Rothenberg, Jerome, 41
Rudd, Roswell, 109
Run DMC, 118
Rushing, Jimmy, 15–16, 38, 108
Salt-N-Pepa, 123
sampling, 122, 131
Sandburg, Carl, 65–69
    The American Songbag, 66–68
Sanders, Ed, 91
"Saturday Night Fish Fry," 87
"Say It Loud, I'm Black and I'm Proud," 95, 98
scat singing, 28, 36–41
"Scat Song, The," 39–40
Schwartz, Delmore, 68, 69
Scott-Heron, Gil, 110–13, 119
scratching, 121–22
Seeger, Pete, 92
sexuality
    in bebop, 87–88
    in jazz, 47–48, 88–89
    in rock 'n' roll, 88
"Shake, Rattle and Roll," 88
Shakur, Tupac, 118, 120, 123, 126
Shepp, Archie, 51, 94
"Sick Man, The," 61
Sidran, Ben, 8, 20
significant tone, 20
Simone, Nina, 35, 97
singing styles. *See* voice
"Sins of Kalamazoo, The" (poem), 66
"Skylark," 77
slang, in jazz, 45–50
slavery
    blues origins in, 14–15
    songs of work and worship, 9–13
Slick, Grace, 91
Sly Stone, 98, 119
Smith, Bessie, 17, 25–27
    analysis of lyrics recorded by, 26–27
    influence on Mezz Mezzrow, 25–26
    jazz conversations and, 21
Smith, Patti, 132

Smith, Stuff, 85
Smith, Trixie, 25
SNCC Freedom Singers, 94
Snoop Doggy Dogg, 118
Songs in the Key of Life (album), 99
soul music, 58, 95
  civil rights movement and, 96–97, 98, 100–101
Soul Stirrers, 89
sound
  in African music, 8
  in jazz, 19–20
  in scat singing, 38
"Speech Rhythms" (essay), 75
Spirits of Rhythm, The, 41
spirituals, 11–12
spoken-word movement, 131–34
Staple Singers, The, 97
"Star Spangled Banner," 98
Starr, Edwin, 97
Stevens, Wallace, "The Sick Man," 61–62
Stewart, Rod, 119
Stills, Steven, 91
Stoller, Mike, 4
"Stormy Weather," 29
storytelling, in jazz, 22–23
"Strange Fruit," 29–30
Strayhorn, Billy
  Duke Ellington and, 32, 35
  "Lush Life," 32–35
Sun Ra, 17
Sun Ra's Arkestra, 109–10
Supremes, The, 91
Sweet Honey in the Rock, 94
swing, 19–20

"Take the A Train," 32
Talking Book (album), 99
Taylor, Billy, 23
Taylor, Cecil, free jazz and, 22, 94
Taylor, Irv, 42
Taylor, Sam "The Man," 107, 108
Tchicai, John, 109
Teagarden, Jack, 85
"Tears for Johannesburg," 57
technology (digital), influence on music and culture, 122–23, 131–37
technology (recording), history of jazz and, 17
Temptations, The, 91, 97
Terry, Clark, 43
Thiele, Bob, 51
"Those Gambler Blues," 67
Timmons, Bobby, 53–54
Tin Pan Alley, 26, 27, 29, 34
tone, in jazz, 20
Too $hort, 118
"Tract" (poem), 77
trance, 131
Treatise on Meter (book), 34
trip hop, 131
"Tryptych — Prayer/Protest/Peace," 56–57
Turner, Big Joe, 88
"Tutuma Is a Big Fine Thing," 4
Tympani Five, 87
Tyner, McCoy, 51

U Roy, 119

Van Gelder, Rudy, 51
vocalese, 43
voice in African music, 7–8
voice in blues, 15

"Wake Up Niggers," 112
Wallace, Sippie, 25
"War," 97

Ward, Brian, 95
Warhol, Andy, 121
Warner Music, 128
Washington, Dinah, 129
Watson, Leo, scat singing and, 38, 40–41
"We Insist!," 57
"We Shall Overcome," 94
Weary Blues, The (album), 107–9
Webb, Chick, 85
Webster, Ben, 15, 17, 21
What's Going On (album), 98
"White Man's Got a God Complex," 112
whites
  dominance in digital culture, 136–37
  record-label owners, 97, 98
  rock 'n' roll and, 87–90, 91
  See also music industry
Whitman, Walt, 63, 66, 68, 84
Who, The, 97
Wilkins, Ernie, 43
William Carlos Williams and the Maternal Muse (book), 76–77
William Carlos Williams and the Meaning of Measure (book), 74–75
Williams, Al, 107
Williams, Cootie, 21
Williams, Elena, 75–77
Williams, Joe, 108
Williams, William Carlos, 73–79
Wilson, Jackie, 88
Wolfe, Bernard, 25
women, hip hop's disrespect for, 124–25, 128
Women of the Blues — The 1930s (album), 3
Wonder, Stevie, 90, 91, 99, 122
Woodyard, Sam, 21
work songs, 10–11
Worrell, Lewis, 109
WWEZ, 50

Xzibit, 123

Yellow Back Radio Broke Down (book), 103
Yes, Mrs. Williams: A Personal History of My Mother (biography), 75
Yo! Bum Rush the Show (album), 123
Young, Lester, 15, 21, 42
Young, Neil, 91

Zappa, Frank, 91
Zukofsky, Louis, 68

Permissions

The publishers have generously given permission to use extended quotations from the following copyrighted works.

From *African Music: A People's Art*, by Francis Bebey. Published by Lawrence Hill Books, an imprint of Chicago Review Press, Inc., USA.

From "Rivers of Babylon," words and music by Brent Dowe, James A. McNaughton, Frank Farian, George Reyam. Copyright © 1978 by Beverley's Records Ltd., administered by Universal /Polygram International Publishing, Inc. (ASCAP) 50.00% International Copyright secured. All rights reserved.

From *Shadow and Act*, by Ralph Ellison. Published by Vintage Books, a division of Random House, Inc.

Three selections from *Really the Blues*, by Mezz Mezzrow and Bernard Wolfe. Copyright © 1946 by Mezz Mezzrow and Bernard Wolfe. Introduction copyright © 1990 by Barry Gifford. All rights reserved. Reprinted by permission of Citadel Press/Kensington Publishing Corp. www.kensingtonbooks.com.

From *Jazz: Myth and Religion*, by Neil Leonard. Reprinted by permission of Oxford University Press.

From "A Fine Romance," words and music by Dorothy Fields, Jerome Kern. Copyright © 1936 by Universal/Polygram International Publishing, Inc. (ASCAP) 100.00% International Copyright secured. All rights reserved.

From "Strange Fruit," by Lewis Allan. Copyright © 1939 (Renewed) by Music Sales Corp. International Copyright Secured. All rights reserved. All rights outside the United States controlled by Edward B. Marks Music Company. Reprinted by permission.

From *Lady Sings the Blues*, by Billie Holiday and William Duffy. Reprinted by permission of Doubleday, a division of Random House, Inc.

From "God Bless the Child," by Billie Holiday, Arthur Herzog, Jr. Copyright © 1941 by Edward B. Marks Music Company. Copyright renewed. Used by permission. All rights reserved.

From "Lush Life," words and music by Billy Strayhorn. Copyright © 1949 (Renewed) by Music Sales Corporation (ASCAP) and Tempo Music, Inc. (ASCAP). International Copyright secured. All rights reserved. Reprinted by permission of Music Sales Corporation.

From "Heebie Jeebies," words and music by Boyd Atkins. Copyright © 1926 Universal/MCA Music Publishing, a division of Universal Studios, Inc. (ASCAP) 100.00% International Copyright secured. All rights reserved.

From *The World of Duke Ellington*, by Stanley Dance. Reprinted with permission of Scribner, a Division of Simon & Schuster. Copyright © 1970 by Stanley Dance.

From " It's the Tune that Counts," words and music by Don Raye, Jan Savitt. Copyright © 1936 by Universal/MCA Music Publishing, a division of Universal Studios Inc. (ASCAP) 100.00% International Copyright secured. All rights reserved.

From "A Love Supreme," by John Coltrane. Copyright © Jowcol Music. Used by permission of Jowcol Music.

From *Chasin' the Train*, by J.C. Thomas. Published by Doubleday, a division of Random House, Inc.

From "Driva' Man," by Oscar Brown, Jr. and Max Roach. Reprinted by permission of Milma Publishing Company.

From *The Collected Poems of Wallace Stevens*, by Wallace Stevens. Copyright © 1954 by Wallace Stevens. Reprinted by permission of Alfred J. Knopf, a division of Random House, Inc.

From the *Collected Poems of Vachel Lindsay, Revised Edition*. (New York: Macmillan, 1925). Used with the permission of Simon & Schuster, Inc.

From "Singing Nigger" from *Cornhuskers*, by Carl Sandburg. Copyright © 1918 by Holt, Rinehart and Winston and renewed 1946 by Carl Sandburg. Reprinted by permission of Harcourt, Inc.

From "Jazz Fantasia" from *Smoke and Steel*, by Carl Sandburg. Copyright © 1920 by Harcourt, Inc. and renewed 1948 by Carl

Sandburg. Reprinted by permission of Harcourt, Inc.

Five selections from *The American Songbag*, by Carl Sandburg. Reprinted by permission of Harcourt Inc.

From *A Time to Speak: The Selected Prose of Archibald McLeish*, by Archibald McLeish. Copyright © 1940 by Archibald McLeish and renewed 1968 by Archibald McLeish. Reprint by permission of Houghton Mifflin Company. All rights reserved.

From "An Exercise," by William Carlos Williams, from *Collected Poems 1939-1962, Volume II*. Copyright © 1962 by William Carlos Williams. Reprinted by permission of New Directions Publishing Corp.

From *William Carlos Williams and the Meaning of Measure*, by Stephen Cushman. Reprinted by permission of Yale University Press.

Selections from *Yes, Mrs. Williams* by William Carlos Williams. Copyright © 1959 by William Carlos Williams. Reprinted by permission of New Directions Publishing Corp.

From *William Carlos Williams and the Maternal Muse*, by Kerry Driscoll (Ann Arbor, MI: UMI Research Press, 1987), pp. 139-40. Reprinted by permission of ProQuest Information and Learning.

From "Tract," by William Carlos Williams, from *Collected Poems, 1909-1939, Volume II*. Copyright © 1938 by New Directions Publishing Corp. Reprinted by permission of New Directions Publishing Corp.

From *The Jack Kerouac Collection*, by Jack Kerouac. Reprinted with permission by Sterling Lord Literistic.

From "Poetry Readings in " The Cellar"" (Fantasy 7002), written by Ralph J. Gleason, performed by Lawrence Ferlinghetti and Kenneth Rexroth. Courtesy of Fantasy, Inc.

From " The Times They are A-Changin,'" by Bob Dylan. Copyright © 1963, 1964 by Warner Bros. Inc and renewed 1991 by Special Rider Music. All rights reserved. International copyright secured. Reprinted by permission.

Four selections from *Everybody Says Freedom: A History of the Civil Rights Movement in Songs and Pictures*, edited by Pete Seeger and Bob Reiser. Copyright © 1989 by Pete Seeger and Bob Reiser. Used by permission of W.W. Norton and Company, Inc.

From *Choice of Colors*, by Curtis Mayfield. Copyright © 1969 (Renewed) Warner-Tamerlane Publishing Corp. All rights reserved. Used by permission of Warner Bros. Publications U.S. Inc., Miami, FL. 33014.

From *Black Fire: An Anthology of African American Writing*, edited by Larry Neal and LeRoi Jones. Reprinted with permission by Sterling Lord Literistic.

From *The Music*, by Imamu Amiri Baraka. Reprinted with permission by Sterling Lord Literistic.

Pages 30-31 from *Understanding the New Black Poetry*, by Stephen Henderson. Copyright © 1972 by Stephen Henderson. Reprinted by permission of HarperCollins Publishers, Inc.

From "Neo-HooDoo Manifesto," by Ishmael Reed. Reprinted by permission of the author.

From "Message to the Messengers," by Gil Scott-Heron. Reprinted with permission by brouhaha Music/TVT Records.

JOHN SOBOL has published hundreds of articles and was the co-writer of *The Genius of Lenny Breau,* which won the 1999 Gemini Award for best Canadian TV arts documentary. As a saxophonist and oral poet, he has given over 1,000 performances in 11 countries since 1979. His CD label, Word of Mouth, has released 8 CDs, including *Blue History* by his own John Sobel Poetry Band. In 1997 his poet trio, AWOL Love Vibe, released a book/CD titled *The Exstatic Almanac.* He is currently the creative director of Globalhood (www.globalhood.net), Canada's only digital lifestyle centre.